Happy B
Earl

2007

Dedicated with love, to my mother.
Mary Rose Crosby Pool
Because Bing was her hero

Me and
Uncle Bing

To Gertrude

With best wishes

Carolyn Schneider

Carolyn Schneider
with Lin Anderson

Copyright © 2005 by Carolyn Schneider.

Library of Congress Number: 2005905418
ISBN : Hardcover 1-4134-9911-2
Softcover 1-4134-9910-4

All rights reserved. No part of this book may be reproduced or transmitted in any form or by any means, electronic or mechanical, including photocopying, recording, or by any information storage and retrieval system, without permission in writing from the copyright owner.

All photographs and graphics contained in this book came from the private collections of *Mary Rose Pool, Susan Crosby,* and other *Crosby* family members, as well as the author. Should there be any unintentional errors, correction or credits that need to be addressed, please contact the author so that proper corrections may be made in all future printings of this book.

This book was printed in the United States of America.

To order additional copies of this book, contact:
Xlibris Corporation
1-888-795-4274
www.Xlibris.com
Orders@Xlibris.com

CONTENTS

ACKNOWLEDGMENTS 9
FOREWORD 11
Chapter 1. BABY FACE 15
Chapter 2. STARDUST 19
Chapter 3. GOING HOLLYWOOD 24
Chapter 4. TOO MARVELOUS FOR WORDS 28
Chapter 5. DEAR HEARTS AND GENTLE PEOPLE 37
Chapter 6. JUST ONE MORE CHANCE 41
Chapter 7. BUT BEAUTIFUL 57
Chapter 8. SWINGING ON A STAR 61
Chapter 9. WHAT'S NEW 68
Chapter 10. STRAIGHT DOWN THE MIDDLE 90
Chapter 11. I'LL BE SEEING YOU 104
Chapter 12. BE CAREFUL, IT'S MY HEART 108
Chapter 13. FAR AWAY PLACES 112
Chapter 14. DON'T FENCE ME IN 117
Chapter 15. ADESTE FIDELIS 126
Chapter 16. REMEMBER ME 134
Chapter 17. BROTHER, CAN YOU SPARE A DIME? .. 140
Chapter 18. THE SINGING HILLS 145
Chapter 19. NOW IS THE HOUR 148
AFTERWORD 153
EPILOGUE 157

ACKNOWLEDGMENTS

For the past several years, my dear husband has suggested that I write this book. I had told him so many stories about my Crosby family, he thought it was high time I put it all down on paper to share with everyone who cared about Uncle Bing and before I have too many more birthdays. We owe him our thanks.

A big thank you to my friend, Linda Crawford, who was instrumental in my finding the Northeastern Nevada Museum and Lin Anderson, both of Elko, Nevada.

Also, I am grateful to our computer guru, Marco Ritzo, who lives next door, (thank goodness).

The wonderful memories you will read about here are all due to my loving family, some of whom I felt were looking over my shoulder as I wrote.

Carolyn

Bing Crosby

FOREWORD

It's been a Long, Long Time

"He died as he lived, and left us his good name."
Epitaph of Captain Nathaniel Crosby

* * *

I am very fortunate to have in my possession the old Crosby family Bible.

I mean the *really old* Crosby family Bible. Hand-written entries from the 19th century are beginning to fade or bleed into the crisp parchment.

When it passed to me upon my mother's death, I marveled that it was still readable at all. On the advice of a knowledgeable librarian, I purchased some acid-free archival paper to place between the pages to preserve them. I was told this is what the Smithsonian Institute uses, so I figured it would be good enough for the Crosbys.

The leather cover on the Bible is somewhat deteriorated, and the binding is nearly gone, so I seldom take it out of its package and I handle it very carefully when I do.

Its poor condition is not simply a consequence of age, but also the result of it being aboard several ships at sea over the years.

Our ancestry includes generations of seafarers. In fact, for a long, long time, our family claim to fame was the intrepid Captain Nathaniel Crosby, a pioneer in trade with the Orient. Captain Nathaniel is buried in Hong Kong.

Which conjures up *The Road to Hong Kong* and brings to mind our other famous relative, Harry and Kate Crosby's fourth son, Harry Lillis "Bing" Crosby.

He was a bit of a pioneer as well as an innovator. Popular entertainment was never the same after Bing came along.

Exactly when he *did* come along has been the subject of more than a little controversy.

For some odd reason, biographers and the media often were given the wrong year, and the wrong day, that Bing Crosby was born.

Finally, undeniable records determined the date to be May 3, 1903 and that raises another point.

Bing and Mary Rose c. 1909.

For years, I have heard stories that there was sibling rivalry between Bing and my mother, his sister, Mary Rose, because my mother's birthday also fell on May 3. She was born three years after Bing.

In fact, some would have it that Bing celebrated his birthday on a different date—May 4—so Mary Rose would have May 3 all to herself.

That's ridiculous. My mother would never have allowed it, in any case. For her, it was a source of pride to be able to let people know that, "Bing and I share the same birthday." It bonded them closely, and they remained close all of their lives.

Bing and mother, then, were both Tauruses, and if you buy into the astrological theory, they exhibited a number of the traits assigned to the Children of the Bull. They were both gregarious and fun-loving; they attracted friends like Irving Berlin attracted royalties.

It's my belief they also both exhibited a streak of immaturity, however. They would blot out their problems in favor of keeping a sunny demeanor at all costs.

Worry could wait for another day. They fell asleep counting their blessings.

I hope I don't owe the Irving Berlin estate a royalty for the preceding line.

My purpose in authoring this book is to perpetuate the memory of my Uncle Bing, and other members of the Crosby family, including my dear mother.

But Bing was the center about which all of us revolved—the Entertainer of the Millennium, according to the BBC. It has been said many times that the mere mention of the word "Bing" anywhere in the world brings instant recognition. There was something in his voice that was friendly, soothing, relaxing. There was never anything boisterous or threatening about it. It had a quality of trust.

This is a book of personal reminiscences. I could never compete with the learned Crosbyphiles who have written so much over the years about Bing Crosby and his career. That is not my intention.

Nor is it my aim to dig up the dirt. If you're looking for titillation or scandal involving my uncle, well, as he used to say, "Aloha on the steel guitar."

I certainly must offer my heartfelt thanks to Bing's fans, who are legion, in the United Kingdom and especially to those in Ireland (where I understand the typical home has photos of the Pope, J.F.K. and Bing, not necessarily in that order) George O'Reilly and Johnny Jones chief among them, as well as Richard Watts in California. They are faithful people who have shown an unwavering love and respect for my uncle. When negative or damaging remarks have been made about him, they have been the first to rally to Uncle Bing's defense, steadfastly championing both the artist and the man.

When I was a child, there was always some smart aleck kid who would ask, "Didn't I hear you were Bing Crosby's niece?"

"That's right," I'd reply.

"I don't believe you!"

"Then why did you ask?"

Nobody asked this time, but I thought I'd answer anyway. Being a part of the Crosby family has been an extraordinary adventure.

Thank you, Uncle Bing.

CAROLYN SCHNEIDER
April, 2004

1. BABY FACE

As I look through my photo albums, I'm reminded of the stories my mother used to tell me about my early childhood. "You were such a good girl," she would say, "I never had to spank or punish you," Well of course I can't swear to that, but I do think that was the impression mother held in her mind and it stayed there for all of her life and mine.

Grandpa Harry holds me while Grandma Kate and mother look on.

The pictures of me from infancy show a pudgy baby with a large round face and rather pretty eyes. As I turn the pages in my album, the photos are of the same little girl, now posing in Japanese pajamas and with a parasol, her hair done in sausage curls, so popular at that time. My guess is that I was about four or five years old now and my mother's darling. She doted on me, I'm happy to say, and acted like I was Shirley Temple. She would show me off to her lady friends and enter me in photo contests. Our radio was constantly playing the latest tunes and mother taught me the words. By the time I was six I could entertain my mother's friends by singing a song, complete with gestures and then take a bow.

I think I was about eight when I had my first train ride. Mother and I were living in San Francisco and we took a taxi to the train station at Third and Townsend streets. I remember it so well because it was such a big event and vary special. We boarded the gray train with orange and red striping, it was called "the Daylight" and it was going to take us safely to Los Angeles and a vacation with my grandparents.

Grandma and Grandpa Crosby were my mother's parents as well as parents to six other children. One of them was Bing Crosby.

It took all day on the train to get to Los Angeles and I was very glad to see my grandparents standing on the platform to greet us. We piled ourselves and the Samsonite luggage into their four door black Buick (they always drove a black Buick) and headed for their home at 4366 Ponca Avenue, which would be our headquarters for the next ten days. The house was in the Taluca Lake district, not for from Uncle Bing's place.

4366 Ponca Avenue

These summer visits to my grandparent's home continued for the next eight or nine years and the pattern of activity during those years remained pretty much the same. The first day was always taken up by mother and Grandma Kate making plans for every day of our vacation. In the beginning, the simple pleasures of staying at my grandparent's was enough for me. Running through the backyard lawn sprinklers on a hot afternoon, going to the Owl drug store for an ice cream cone, going around the block on my roller skates that I'd brought along, or capturing lady bugs in an empty jam jar. As I grew older and less satisfied with those basic childhood sports, the plans for entertainment were up-graded by mother and grandma. The next rung in the ladder included daily jaunts to go swimming at one of the clubs our family belonged to. Then dates were made to go and see some of our other relatives that lived in Los Angeles. Several of them had pools so sometimes we didn't need to go to the club for a swim. By the time I was ten or eleven I realized this Crosby family that I was a member of, had some special features. For example, a couple of my uncles seemed to be very important men and the kind of work they did was called "show business." They lived in great big fancy houses and had people there that bought them food or drinks, just like in a restaurant. Pretty ritzy, I thought.

About the time I reached my thirteenth birthday, our summer trip to Los Angeles and my grandparents was at its peak. Now the plans were made to go to Paramount Studios and have lunch in the commissary, which was not an elegant place at all, but more like a coffee shop, diner, or cafeteria. It was a big deal for me however, because the chances were very good that I would see some movie stars. If not, it at least would be full of actors in costumes and make-up. Being there was pure joy for me. I ate my meal very slowly in order to make the lunch hour last longer and give me a chance to look over the entire room, looking for stars. Even if I came up empty in the celebrity department, the outing was worth it, just to see people dressed as Roman soldiers, or a Spanish dancer or a princess. What a lucky girl I was.

The following year or so really brought home to me the fact that my Uncle Bing was himself a real movie star. Mother and I were allowed to go on the set at Paramount and watch him making "Emperor's Waltz." More and more I noticed Uncle Bing's voice coming out of the radio and whenever we were in Los Angeles, I would see his image at different places around town, like the Brown Derby restaurant, even on the cover of the menu. There was simply no denying it; my uncle had made the big time. While growing up, I was never jealous or resentful after those trips to Los Angeles, that we didn't live like our wealthy relatives. Rather, I felt like I'd been to the movies and it was time to go home.

When I entered high school, word got around pretty fast that I was Bing's niece, I don't know who spilled the beans but I instantly had friends. It really didn't matter, because like most teenagers, I felt awkward and was about a quart low in the self esteem department.

I had told my school counselor that I would not be going on to college, because I was quite sure my mother couldn't afford it. I thought I would be joining the workforce and get some kind of job, although at this point I had absolutely no marketable skills. But when you're young and immature, all things seem possible.

It was a total surprise to me therefore, that on graduation day in June my mother informed me that I should plan to enroll in college that following September. I had no idea how to do this, I was caught completely off-guard. However, mother explained that she had talked to Uncle Bing and he offered to pay my college tuition for the next four years. Mother never had the opportunity for higher education herself, but apparently she wanted me to have every advantage for the future.

Bing, upper left, in Roman Collar

2. STARDUST

I graduated from college, to the wide-eyed pleasure of my mother, in 1954, donning cap and gown and solemnly accepting my degree in drama and theater arts, which I was convinced, would lead to a career in show business.

Convinced right along with me, were my classmates who had trod the boards in the San Jose State College Drama Department, and approximately several thousand other would-be James Deans and Natalie Woods scattered throughout this great nation, who were being slipped a sheepskin at approximately the same time. In short, nobody lacked for competition.

I didn't have the looks or the figure of a showgirl or starlet, so it's just as well that I concentrated on being a comedienne. I had enjoyed some limited success in school productions which encouraged me to try the "big time," not in New York, but Hollywood.

I had a bit of a head start on the field, however. My mother, I might as well go ahead and say "stage mother" in the interests of accuracy, had me belting out contemporary hits for family gatherings since I was just out of diapers. So I had all that going for me. And then I had the Theory of Relativity on my side.

Well, it's more than theory. It's proven gospel truth that, if you want to get into show business, or any other business, for that matter, an understanding or at least long-suffering family member who can throw open a couple of doors for you is a fantastic break.

In my case, the Theory of Relativity revolved around my uncle. He'd been out there pitching songs since vaudeville and probably knew more about showbiz than just about anyone on earth. In later years, when time had passed sufficiently for his contributions to be evaluated and appreciated, he would even be called the "first multimedia star."

I just called him my Uncle Bing.

You, on the other hand, are welcome to call me a little slow on the uptake, because I was all of 10 or 11 years of age before I realized just exactly what a world figure Bing Crosby was. I was too busy being a kid to have much time to dwell on far-flung concepts like that.

I knew that Uncle Bing was in show business, because it seemed like he was on the radio all the time around our house. I didn't quite grasp that he was on the radio all the time around everybody else's house, too.

Once in awhile, a thick 78 r.p.m. record would arrive at our door in Alameda, California, because Uncle Bing always dutifully sent my mother one of the first pressed copies of his new release, bearing a label reading **SAMPLE, NOT FOR SALE**. Mother would put the record on the phonograph, sit down, and get all moony-eyed marveling at what her remarkable brother had done this time around. In later years, one of her favorites was "True Love."

Uncle Bing's voice was a spiritual tonic to mother. She was in no respects a wealthy woman, although she would do quite well in real estate later in her life. Mother's marriage to my father had ended in divorce, leaving her to raise me alone, while she honed the secretarial skills that just barely got us by. It was a difficult life, but she never lost the gregarious spirit and wonderful sense of humor that had always made her the light of her family.

And she had the sure knowledge that her big brother would be there for her. "From the time he was a little boy," she said, "you could always hear

Uncle Bing, mid 1950's

him coming down the street. He was always singing or whistling." She thought it was a comforting sound, and it was indeed precisely that for uncounted millions during the Great Depression, World War II, and into the years well beyond.

Singer Peggy Lee touched on that comforting appeal in what I think is a great description of the sheer magic my uncle was capable of: "He didn't really know what great things his singing did for others," she said. "Or what a wonderful influence his personality had on people. There is a certain security just even thinking about Bing."

It was a slam-dunk, therefore, that mother would pick up the phone and call her musical brother, requesting his hard-won advice on how to get her star-struck daughter launched into show business in Hollywood.

The Crosby family at home in Spokane, WA. Kay, Kate, Mary Rose and Harry Are in the back row; Bing and Ted crouch in front.

Whatever advice Uncle Bing offered would be adhered to quite fanatically, because, in her eyes, Bing was her hero who could never do wrong, even when he did. Mother's adulation of Bing began at a very early age, perhaps on that memorable day when he "wiped up the school yard" with a boy named Jim Turner who had called her "Fatty." Such was Bing's impact even then that the victim of the young crooner's wrath turned around and asked Mary Rose to a school dance. Or so the story goes.

Although he was world-famous for being relaxed, except when cheering a racehorse down the stretch or defending his baby sister's honor, Uncle Bing immediately volunteered to sign on as associate producer of this career plan for his niece. I think he probably liked the idea of giving a break to a sweet kid he had known since babyhood, a girl with the very good taste to have inherited her mother's idolization of him.

I'm not saying he wouldn't have breathed a good, long, sigh after he dropped the receiver on mother's call, probably shaking his head and musing with a chuckle, "So Cookie wants to be a star."

Everybody called me "Cookie" in those days. I believe it was an unwritten law that, if you were a Crosby, you had to have a nickname. Mother's was "Posie."

Of course my uncle's roster of them was the stuff of legend.

"Bing" itself was a nickname, as just about everyone knows. And "Bing" morphed into things like "El Bingo" and "Der Bingle." Tommy Dorsey coined "The Groaner" in an affectionate backhanded tribute to Bing's singing style.

Whatever you called him, you knew that when you called *on* him, he'd give your entreaty a decent hearing. "Whenever I had problems," mother once recalled, "I always went to Bing and he calmed me down and advised me what I should do." She had a great deal of respect for him and was fully aware that his experience in most matters was greater than hers.

By the same token, mother was the Crosby that other family members turned to if they needed help convincing Bing that some course of action was in his best interest. His brothers Everett and Larry, who handled Bing's affairs, often utilized her for this purpose. Naturally, she just loved that.

I probably shouldn't have bothered him with my career goals, but since Uncle Bing had unloaded some serious coin for my college education, I'm sure he looked at assisting me on my own private Road To Utopia not just as a labor of love, but as an opportunity to personally see to it there was some sort of rebound on his investment. He was a big star, but unlike most big stars, he was also a canny businessman

"Let me make a few calls," Bing told mother.

She thanked him, and then asked how he was doing. That produced a little more subdued conversation. At that point, Uncle Bing was still getting used to being a widower with four sons to look after. Let's face it, in the mid-1950s, or any other era, raising four teenage boys is a full-time job that very few would have the courage to apply for.

From the second mother hung up the phone, I lived in nail-biting suspense, praying God would suddenly speed up time so that everything happened instantly, like Minute Maid Orange Juice, another of my uncle's many pursuits.

It was just a couple of days later, although it seemed like a month or so to me, that Bing telephoned mother with a plan for my future. I don't know who was more excited about my going to Los Angeles, Tinsel Town, Gollywood, or La-La Land, as it was sometimes called, my mother or me. To set a goal for yourself in life and have a chance to reach it, that brass ring, what a fabulous opportunity I was about to take advantage of, thanks to Uncle Bing. He told her he had made some inquiries for a reputable domicile which would be suitable for a single girl in the big city, and he'd learned the ideal residence was a place called the Hollywood

Studio Club, which was operated by the YWCA, and had been seen to its completion by Mrs. Cecil B. DeMille, no less.

Staunch Catholic that he was, I think Uncle Bing liked the idea of a hostelry with at least a nodding acquaintance with the Ten Commandments.

The noted architect Julia Morgan designed the club, which is now on the National Register of Historic Places. Discovering your old stomping grounds on that list is proof of the realities of age, but I hasten to add that the club had been sheltering ingenues for nearly 30 years by the time I showed up.

Uncle Bing informed mother the Studio Club's residents were an eclectic roster, indeed. In addition to actresses, there were singers, dancers, comediennes, writers, script girls, make-up artists, secretaries, producers, and almost any other Hollywood job description you could think of. Both Marilyn Monroe and Ayn Rand were Studio Club alumni.

Now, *that's* eclectic.

Kim Novak lived there, too.

The Hollywood Studio Club.

I was just dying to get in.

The knotty little problem was that they had no immediate vacancies. Not even for Father O'Malley's niece. This was a major disappointment for me, and a slight one for the good padre himself, but the Studio Club assured Uncle Bing that I would be put on the waiting list.

And it I wouldn't be homeless in the interim. My uncle decreed that I was to come to Los Angeles and live in his elaborate digs at 594 Mapleton Drive, while I waited for the Hollywood Studio Club to come to its senses. What a grand idea!

3. GOING HOLLYWOOD

Number Five Ninety-Four was an attractive Tudor-style house located in the Holmby Hills-Beverly Hills section of Los Angeles. Uncle Bing had settled into the residence many years before with his wife, my Aunt Dixie—and their four rambunctious sons.

While Mapleton Drive, to this day boasts that same number, a different house now sits atop the spacious lot, Aaron Spelling's place. The house I remember exists only in photographs and memories. If the photos are a little bit faded, the memories are vivid.

I expected that I would have a 594 Mapleton Drive of my own very shortly, since I had come to Los Angeles trailing a blizzard of favorable publicity from my college theater days. Actually it was more like a drizzle, but my uncle had taught me, along with the rest of the Western World, to ac-cen-tu-ate the positive.

Who was I to argue with that kind of logic?

So at the end of that summer, American Airlines set me down at the Los Angeles airport, where I was met by Louis Serpe, Uncle Bing's stocky chauffeur, who was piloting the latest in a seemingly never-ending series of the giant black Cadillacs my uncle liked. I realized that Louis and I were both dressed in suit, hat and gloves that day. "Full-livery," as they say.

It was good to see Louis's familiar face, and he quickly put me at ease with his breezy charm as we crossed the miles to Beverly Hills. Like my uncle, Louis was one of those fellows who could and did ramble on pleasantly about almost anything, and I was happy to find my nervousness quickly drowned in the stream of conversation flowing from the front seat.

I asked Louis to show me Rodeo Drive and to alert me instantly if he saw any movie stars. Apparently they were all elsewhere that day.

We eventually rolled up the opulent driveway at Uncle Bing's place and were met by Miss Georgie Hardwicke, the housekeeper, whom I had known before and like everyone else, slightly feared.

What a character.

Georgie's whole attitude, sunrise to sunset, was busy. She zinged around the house like a careening bullet, pausing frequently to wipe her nose with the ever-present Kleenex she kept tucked up in her sleeve. I don't know why she wiped her nose so often, she took her job seriously, so maybe it was that whole "nose to the grindstone" thing. Perhaps her nasal issues stemmed from the sheer speed and altitude she needed to maintain in order to keep Mr. Crosby's place running smoothly. In any case, she was always in high gear; the nose didn't slow her down a bit.

594 Mapleton Drive

Until fairly recently, Georgie's duties had included serving as Governess to Bing and Dixie's brood and good lord that had been sheer terror! I always thought it was no accident that Georgie's posture, determinedly bent forward, resembled a woman walking into a hurricane. She'd certainly weathered her share.

Louis and Georgie fished my vintage Samsonite luggage from the trunk of the Cadillac and we strolled through the big doors and into the foyer of Uncle Bing's home. I felt the wayward butterflies return. What the devil had I gotten myself into? Did I really think I ought to be in pictures?

I tried my darndest to e-lim-in-ate the negative and found the palpitations easing a bit when I reassured myself that I had quite a lot of kin for moral support here in southern California. And I certainly had one heck of a place to stay; this fine home that Uncle Bing's hit songs and undeniable box office magic had built. It was a far cry from the humble abode that mother and I called home, but then I wasn't a well-known celebrity.... Yet. If the house seemed huge to me when I visited there as a child, this time it felt more like my size, the rooms were not quite so overwhelming.

The foyer led to a curved staircase, which rose gracefully to the second floor and a sumptuous bedroom suite. Beautifully decorated, it sported white organdy curtains, and appointments of soft pink and white. There was a spacious closet, a table and desk, nightstands and lamps, a chaise longue, an expensively-mirrored dressing area, and those dainty chairs that ladies of the day liked to sit in when visiting.

This had been Aunt Dixie's suite.

Dixie Lee Crosby

4. TOO MARVELOUS FOR WORDS

I was just a small child when I first made the acquaintance of Aunt Dixie, back in those carefree days when I thought her husband worked awfully hard singing songs for my mother.

As I matured a bit, and grew to know her better, I found that Dixie always made me feel comfortable and at ease. She was a person with absolutely no pretense at all. Salty, caring and fun, she was very much a realist in a town where reality was way down on the list of things to do today. Her veneer of sarcastic humor was legendary. She wouldn't pull, or telegraph, her punches with you, and she expected you to treat her in the same fashion. In that respect, as in others, she was one of a new breed of women born with the twentieth century, a sometimes uneasy mix of femininity and toughness. "We could always count on her for the truth about ourselves," Uncle Bing once said.

And wow, was she beautiful

The biographers tell us that Uncle Bing and Aunt Dixie met in 1929, when she was just 18 years of age. She was an ingenue at Fox; he was playing clubs in Los Angeles with Paul Whiteman's band. They were married a year later, in the fall of 1930.

Dixie the starlet

Dixie's publicity photo

By the time Dixie and Bing were wed, she had already made a few well-received pictures and was, a bit to Bing's chagrin, better known than he was. In fact, the newspaper headlines announcing the nuptials were uniformly along the lines of "DIXIE LEE MARRIES SINGER". Bing maintained one of them actually pronounced to the world that, "WELL KNOWN FOX MOVIE STAR MARRIES BING CROVENY."

Dixie poses for the camera

When Bing's career began taking off and she began having her children, Aunt Dixie left the bright lights behind and became a much more private person, and it was that woman that I came to know.

Bing said Dixie had no qualms about leaving show business. The rampant fakery exhausted her, and she most certainly could not stomach the insincerity that was forced upon her, those terrible occasions when she would have to smile sweetly for someone when she would have rather have stuck out her tongue. "She tried to do these things, but she died inside as she did them," Bing said.

I never heard her called Wilma, which was her real name. Wilma Winifred Wyatt. Despite the charming sound, I think it was just plain "Dixie" right from the very beginning, back in Harriman, Tennessee, where she was born. Her father's appearance always reminded me of Col. Sanders of fried chicken fame. Luckily, she did not resemble him.

Dixie with a favorite pooch

She was petite, only five-foot-three, but she had a force of personality that people noticed instantly, and her bold inner spirit found its expression in many ways. She could, for instance, caress a tune nearly as well as her husband could. Bing said in fact that when it came to selling a song, "She had no equal."

Bing and Dixie

One physical trait that set her apart was a vision problem, which required that she wear unusual glasses, tinted robin's egg blue. I had never seen any like that before in my life. Few in those days had. They weren't at all common back before designer sunglasses became all the rage. One of her twin sons, Dennis, inherited her condition and later wore the same sort of lenses, but by then people thought it was just a matter of, as they say today, stylish.

Bing and Dixie poolside

A smoker, Dixie used a cigarette holder and looked very elegant handling it. Her voice was smoky as well, low and raspy and very appealing to both men and women.

When you visited her in that suite of rooms upstairs, you would often find her dressed in a peignoir set, an elegant, flowing nightgown and robe. It was something she felt comfortable in and it didn't seem at all surprising that she would greet you wearing it. Sometimes, in the interest of drama, the outfit would be accented with mirabou.

As short as she was, she gave the impression of having some height. She favored wearing high-heeled, backless slippers, some of them covered with fur or feathers.

You might say that some of her outfits were flamboyant or even eccentric. If you did, Dixie would fix you with that gaze of hers that said, "Tough luck. This is me. Take it or leave it."

A guest, Aunt June and Aunt Dixie.

As Bing's fame grew to worldwide proportions—to the point where even I couldn't miss it—going out to shop became less a pleasure for Dixie than it was a chore. Therefore, the latest styles were brought to her by the upscale stores such as: I. Magnin, Bullocks Wilshire, or Sax Fifth Avenue. Salespeople from the stores would make appointments and come by the house trailing a couple of racks of the latest threads plus a model or two and display what they had to offer this month.

The same was true for her hair stylist. Dixie didn't go to the beauty shop, the beauty shop came to her. As a youngster, I remember seeing the large hair-dryer-on-wheels in her dressing area, and thinking that was the sheer ultimate in being a classy lady.

Dixie and three of her boys: Gary, Phil and Dennis.

On those occasions when mother and I would call on her, Dixie got a real kick out of seeing me try on some of her clothes. "Carolyn!" she would call out, "I wonder how you'd look in my silver fox!"

It was an order, not a question, and served as my cue to pop into her dressing room, later re-emerging to model the garment for Dixie and mother.

"Oh, honey! That's YOU!" Dixie would cry, and she and mother would dissolve in laughter, usually calling out to Georgie to rustle up a couple of cocktails to dissolve them further.

Dixie visits the military school

While she fully enjoyed her numerous perks, Dixie was a giver, too. As a result, she particularly loved Christmas, even before her husband started crooning about it all the time.

She favored a certain line of custom glassware with a silver band and over the years each family member would receive a gift from the line at Christmas.

A pitcher and set of glasses were under Crosby family trees one year, followed on successive Christmases by a salad bowl and plates, an Irish coffee set, a chip and dip arrangement and a shrimp cocktail set. Cocktail glasses short and tall were also added to the silver-bedecked ensemble.

It all got to be so much that, one year; my Uncle Bob took Bing aside and asked if a new gift line might be introduced. "Confidentially, Bing," Bob said, "we're up to our ass in glass." "Fine," Bing answered, "I'll have my secretary take you off the list," and he did. Bob and his wife never received another gift from him at Christmas.

Dixie and Bing had such a large group of friends and family that their gift list was horrendously long, but Aunt Dixie filled it every year. There were so many packages to prepare that Dixie would have to hire a couple of women to come in to wrap and mail packages. There is a kid in all of us, and Dixie's was in full view each and every Christmas.

Over the years, I received some lovely gifts from Dixie's Workshop. I recall a medal one Christmas, a gold pen and pencil set the next, all engraved, "Love from Bing and Dixie."

By the same token, "the Bing's", that was their nickname as a couple, received so many Christmas gifts that it literally took them two or three days to open them all.

No, I'm *not* kidding.

While that might seem an enviable situation to those of us who complete our unwrapping by noon at the latest, Bing and Dixie found themselves simply overwhelmed by the stacks of gifts they would receive. For instance, I remember seeing a lovely set of monogrammed towels from Bob and Dolores Hope. When Bing sang about "presents on the tree," I imagine he was half wondering whether he and Dixie would someday have to add on to the house to accommodate them.

Dixie's generosity was hardly confined to the holidays. I recall a grade school summer vacation when mother and I were making our regular visit to Los Angeles. Bing and Dixie had rented a place at Malibu, right on the beach.

We were lunching there one day, Dixie attired in one of the gorgeous two-piece white bathing suits from her voluminous collection of them, when I told my aunt how very much I admired her watch. It was rose gold and festooned with rubies, but not ostentatious by any means. Still, to my eyes as a child and not a person of wealth, that watch was the living end.

The next thing you know, Dixie had slipped it off and was dangling it in front of me, grinning broadly and saying, "Live it up, honey! Wear it while you're here today". I couldn't believe my good fortune.

Living it up was short-lived, however. My mother had a genuine fit when she saw me on the beach making castles out of sand while sporting Aunt Dixie's gorgeous watch. I had to take it off and give it back, right that second.

Dixie lived in a house of men and boys, she never had a daughter of her own. I think maybe that's why she shared so much with me in my childhood years. I remember many occasions when I would go padding off into her dressing area and simply marvel at her sensational clothes. I'd slide one mirrored section of her closet doors open and that would contain all of her skirts; slide back the next door and it would be filled with blouses. It was like a department store! Two dozen hanging there! For the most part, these things were of a "tailored" style, no ruffles or provocative outfits for this lady.

Dixie, Bing and the four boys.

And the next compartment would be her dresses, and then her coats, and then there was the "secret" panel, a mystery she nevertheless clued me in on, which concealed the wall safe where she kept her fine jewelry.

One of the most thoughtful gifts I ever received came from Dixie, back when I was a senior in high school.

Dixie and mother were talking on the phone one day when Dixie inquired what I might like for Christmas. Mother informed her I would be going to the prom that season, and I didn't yet have a dress for the occasion.

As you might imagine, Dixie found that unacceptable.

In short order, a big box arrived from Los Angeles. Aunt Dixie had sent me my prom dress. It was as stylish as she was, a sparkling white with rhinestones on it. A real knockout! I couldn't have been more excited, nor more grateful. When I tried the dress on, it fit perfectly. As I twirled around in front of the mirror, it seemed to have a magical quality. I'd never owned anything so beautiful.

There was a bit of a problem, however. This gown was strapless. And I went to Notre Dame High School, which meant the dress would have to pass muster with both my mother and a whole cadre of nuns.

As a result, there were some alterations made. A dressmaker was assigned to craft a matching bolero jacket, which I discarded the second I hit the dance floor.

Dixie was pleased that her gift had been a smash at the prom. She so loved dances and parties, they brought out both her gregarious nature, and her mischievous sense of humor. One year, mother received a beautifully engraved invitation alerting her that Dixie was tossing Bing a surprise birthday party.

On it was noted, "Black Tie."

In parentheses, Dixie had added: "*That'll* surprise him!"

Grandma Kate

5. DEAR HEARTS AND GENTLE PEOPLE

When I arrived to stay at the Mapleton Drive house in 1955, Aunt Dixie had been gone for three years and her suite was occupied by Uncle Bing's mother, my Grandma Kate.

After the death of his dad, Bing had invited his mother to live with him because he wanted to take care of her and wanted her close by. But having Grandma Kate around was a bit of a tonic for him as well, strong medicine certainly.

And her presence surely kept Uncle Bing grounded. It's hard to believe your own fawning publicity when the strong-minded woman you've known since the moment of birth is rattling around your house saying things like, "You're not really going out wearing THAT, are you?"

Uncle Bing's taste in clothes, especially those loud Hawaiian shirts he made famous, was never a particularly strong suit with the ladies, including his mother.

Grandma knew her son had become world renowned, but that didn't keep her from dishing out some down to earth opinions or advice. When Uncle Bing's book "Call Me Lucky" was published, she asked him where in the world did he get that title and followed up with this remark, "luck had nothing to do with your success. It was the prayers of your Irish mother and the Poor Clare nuns that got you where you are today!" Uncle Bing smiled, gave her a kiss on the cheek and handed her a first edition copy.

Bing's Irish heritage came from Grandma Kate, and she was most assuredly not your stereotypical colleen with the lilting laughter, although she did have such a pleasant singing voice in the church choir that grandpa nicknamed her "Birdie."

She was a no-nonsense, staunchly conservative woman, who had little use for gray areas, but with a brood of seven children, she surely had to run a tight ship. In addition, she had to keep a tight rein on the purse strings. Grandpa always maintained a steady job but his salary fell a bit short of what was needed for this family of nine. Therefore, as a young married woman, Grandma Kate made hats at home for what she called her "pin money, a woman should always have some money set aside in her sock," she advised me. Another pearl of wisdom: "a woman who will tell her age will tell anything."

Kate abided by the rules of her Catholic faith. She was so proud of Uncle Bing portraying a priest and winning an Oscar for it, yet! It was perhaps a bit of wishful thinking on her part. She had hoped and prayed that one of her five sons would enter the priesthood, every Irish mother's dream, I suppose.

And in grandmother's case, if one of the boys took the vows, she would still have four spares around to provide her with grandchildren.

The only occasions when she deviated from the teachings of Rome, that I recall, were the days when she would have Louis drive her over to visit her Scottish friend Maggie Thompson, who would read her tea leaves. There were a few other things that Grandma believed in that were not sanctioned by the Pope, but apparently were part of some sort of Irish tradition. Like horse race gambling. And she deemed that acceptable.

Besides, "Santa Anita" sounds sort of religious.

Bing's father was of stern British ancestry, yet he was jovial, easygoing and devilish. The cliché is very apt in his case: his eyes had a Santa Claus twinkle. He was a bit rotund, wore round steel rimmed glasses and always sported a vest with a gold pocket watch on a chain. After breakfast each day, before leaving the table, I remember that he would take out his watch to check the time, making him look somewhat like a railroad conductor. He passed his given name, Harry, along to his fourth son, together with the breezy nonchalance that Uncle Bing would make famous around the world.

Another of my uncles, the noted bandleader Bob Crosby, told me once that he never remembered his mother kissing him, and described his father as more of a brother or a pal to him, not a stern father.

Uncle Bob, the baby of the brood, also recalled that his father was a particularly soft touch for the tireless workers in the sales industry. "My lord, we had every new household appliance, for a week," Bob said. "Then when Dad couldn't make the next week's payment, it had to go back."

So Harry and Kate were the two genetic cards that Bing had to draw from, and their diametrically-opposed parenting styles couldn't help but have affected his own parenting, and the way he made decisions and set standards for himself and others.

His brothers Everett, Larry, Ted and Bob, and sisters Kay and Mary Rose, also inherited their share of Harry and Kate's imperfections, but Bing was the one displaying them on a literal world stage.

From Kate, then, came the care he exhibited with money after a somewhat rocky fiscal start. Kate also pounded home the Catholic certainty that both divorce and drink were grievous evils.

But Bing's mother had seen all those household appliances disappear, so she could offer sunnier counsel: keep the faith, better days are always ahead. In that regard, I can still hear Grandma reciting one of her time-tested nuggets of advice: "There's nothing wrong with being poor, it's just damned inconvenient." It's possible then, that as a result of his mother's warnings, Uncle Bing established a certain philosophy regarding money. By the time I was old enough to understand such things, I learned through my mother, that while he was not some selfish miser, Uncle Bing was not a fool either, when it came to the subject of money. I think he was generous when the situation called for it and was particularly tender-hearted when it came to the women in our family, as evidenced by his Last Will and Testament. Uncle Bing left cash bequests to myself and three other nieces, no nephews, as well as my mother, a female cousin of his and a secretary. Maybe Grandma told him we were the "weaker sex". Fancy that!

Always generous when it came to Grandma, sometime in the late 1950's as I recall, Uncle Bing gave his mother an all expense paid trip to Europe. Grandma took Aunt Kay along as her companion. It must have a mixed blessing for my aunt, because she dare not have a cocktail or light a cigarette in front of her mother.

It didn't bother him that people joked about his wealth. As a matter of fact, Uncle Bing tells this story about being in a taxi coming from the airport one day. The driver kept staring at him in his rear view mirror. Finally the cabbie said, "Did anyone ever tell you that you look like Bing Crosby?"

"Whoa! Not me," Bing replied, "who would want to look like *him*—he's an ugly looking guy."

"But I bet you wouldn't mind having his money," said the driver.

I witnessed one out-of-character incident of extravagance on Grandma Kate's part, which occurred while I was living at 594 Mapleton. She and I had gone shopping on Rodeo Drive, in Beverly Hills, and she asked Louis to stop at an exclusive haberdashery, where the clerk greeted her by name.

She bought a handsome pair of silk pajamas and ordered Uncle Bing's monogram be put on the pocket.

The bill came to more that $100.00.

I was shocked!

Grandma Kate must have noticed my dumbfounded reaction. "I don't ordinarily spend this much for a gift," she said, "but these are for Bing."

While Grandma Kate laid down the law, Grandpa Harry on the other hand peppered Bing with lessons centered about enjoying life and keeping a kind and understanding heart. An Olympia brewery bookkeeper for much of his working life, Harry also advised that a little nip now and then never hurt anybody.

Grandpa and Uncle Bing: the two Harry Crosbys. Bing inherited the happy-go-lucky nonchalance he displayed on the screen from his father. Grandma Kate passed down a little more stern stuff to her crooning son.

That advice backfired on him occasionally. I recall one time he and Bing went to a baseball game and Harry arrived home late, well, early, to find Kate wailing like McNamara's Band, angry and suspicious that Harry had consumed more than a few beers at the game. There was no way Harry could dispute that point, especially vertically, so Kate locked him out and no manner of pleading could get her to let him inside. Bing took his father to *his* home for the night.

Adjacent to grandma's quarters at 594 Mapleton was what I guess you would call the quintessential "man's man's" retreat, a combination den and office, with a dressing room and bathroom and a small bedroom set-up.

Here it was all dark woods, hunter greens, the paraphernalia of the sportsman, a very masculine area smelling deliciously of a recently-smoked pipe. This was Uncle Bing's suite.

Down the hall was headquarters for Bing and Dixie's quartet of sons. They had flown this spacious coop by the time I arrived, but in their younger years they had slept two to a room and had a large playroom to, well, be boys in. There were tables set up with games and puzzles on them, a pool table, a radio, a place to play records, which one of them, Gary, was then in the process of making, as he tried to follow in the enormous tracks of his father.

Gary, in his "heartthrob" days.

6. JUST ONE MORE CHANCE

I am quite often asked about Bing and Dixie's sons, my cousins Gary, Phillip, Dennis and Lindsay. The questioning was particularly hurtful in the wake of Gary's 1983 book *Going My Own Way*, which characterized my uncle as a distant, cold, disciplinarian, and Aunt Dixie as a helpless, withdrawn alcoholic. It was a sad book, written, I believe, partially because of the need for quick money and it had a terrible, terrible impact.

Gary and I at play as children.

41

That impact, however, came mostly through what was written *about* the book. Writers, particularly the tabloid writers, took Gary's tales of what he said was his father's harsh code of discipline, and splashed them onto lurid covers, conveniently leaving out passages like this one:

Bing visits with the four boys at rehearsal

"The old man believed what he believed, and he thought he was doing right," Gary wrote. "He wasn't any tougher than a lot of fathers of his generation. And a lot of kids can handle that kind of upbringing without any difficulty. It was too bad that my brothers and I didn't buy it and turn out the way he wanted. That would have made it very comfortable for everyone."

"But whatever the reasons, we didn't. Linny and the twins clammed up like a shell. I bulled my neck and fought him tooth and nail all the way down the line, to my own destruction. The discipline just didn't work with us."

Despite the leavening effects of such *mea culpas*, the damage had been done. Most people didn't read the book at all, they read *about* the book. And what they read was deeply troubling. It certainly was for all of us in the family.

As young adults—Phil, Dennis and myself. Lindsay kneels in the foreground.

Gary never told me about any kind of heavy handed discipline from his father, I certainly never witnessed anything like that, so what he described in his book was a complete shock to me.

Gary, Lindsay, Phil and Dennis.

Gary's attack on his father caused an especially serious rift between him and his brother Phil, who lashed out in an interview at the time, "My dad was not the monster my lying brother said he was, he was strict, but my father never beat us black and blue and my brother Gary was a vicious, no-good liar for saying so."

"I have nothing but fond memories of dad," Phil continued, "going to studios with him, family vacations at our cabin in Idaho, boating and fishing with him. To my dying day, I'll hate Gary for dragging dad's name through the mud. He wrote it out of greed. He wanted to make money and knew that humiliating our father and blackening his name was the only way he could do it. He knew it would generate a lot of publicity and that was the only way he could get his ugly, no-talent face on television and in the newspapers. My dad was my hero. I loved him very much. And he loved all of us too, including Gary. He was a great father."

Bing and Lindsay on a movie set

The four boys visit Bing at work

Gary's memoir was just more trouble in what had already been a troublesome life for Bing and Dixie's sons. I had grown up with them, played with them when we were kids and socialized with them occasionally throughout their lives. We had some good times, but there always seemed to be one disaster or another lurking just around the bend, often with a stop first at a nearby cocktail lounge or Beverly Hills party.

There's no question in my mind that they were deeply affected by their parents' stormy marriage. In any event, I believe there was always love between Bing and Dixie and it was manifest in her final days.

Publicity shot of the boys: Gary, Lindsay, Dennis and Phil.

Bing on his way to fame and fortune

Mother told me that Dixie had threatened divorce over Bing's behavior in the early days of their union, when Bing was drinking and staying out late. The situation was reversed years later, when Dixie began drinking heavily.

Unlike her stretched-to-the-limit husband, I believe Dixie was quite often at loose ends for something to do. Georgie ran the household and there were other servants to do the day-to-day chores.

I saw her as a woman who was deep-down shy, hiding her insecurities with wisecracks, although they were always wonderfully smart ones. An introvert behaving like an extrovert, the cocktails helped her deal with the boredom and loneliness that came with Bing's celebrity status.

I have the notion that she was always uncomfortable around his fans, but she did enjoy going to the horse races with Bing. The couple seldom went nightclubbing, or to the Hollywood premieres. In fact, they weren't seen together in public very much at all, in the later years.

Bing fishing at his Rising River ranch

Bing hunting with his favorite Labrador

Dixie didn't play golf, nor did she share Bing's love of hunting and fishing. So he went off adventuring by himself or with his buddies. She did travel to their ranch at Elko, Nevada, occasionally, but that sort of bucolic life just wasn't my aunt's cup of tea, or vodka tonic.

Bing the hunter

Bing and Dixie once made a record together, on one side "A Fine Romance," on the other, "Let's Call the Whole Thing Off." At the time, we in the family felt there was more truth than poetry whirling on the spindle there, and we were more than a little perplexed about why they had made the recording. The whole project seemed to quite uncomfortably spill the beans about what Bing and Dixie's lives had become, in their *his and hers* suites. Bing was firmly against divorce and never wanted to appear to condone it. A couple of stories circulated through our family, one of them had it that the wife of a nephew was applying for a job at a studio and they asked Bing to give her a reference. But when he learned she had been divorced, he declined to give it. I know at the time of his death, Bing excluded one of my cousins from his Will and the talk was that he had done that because she was divorced. However, I was divorced as well and yet he left me a nice bequest. Go figure!

The boys came of age in the midst of their parents' marital turmoil.

All of the boys started college, but none of them finished, apparently feeling little pressure to earn a living or to make money, since their financial lives were for the most part in the hands of money managers. They were teenagers when Aunt Dixie passed away in 1952, she left them some of her own wealth, but it didn't last forever. Generally speaking, I guess, without them adding to it, they simply kept spending the principal.

As the boys grew older, moved out of the house and started their own lives away from each other as well as their parents, they decided to get together and form a quartet to launch a career in nightclubs, with an eye on Las Vegas. The news was greeted with some substantial, and very favorable, press. They even made the cover of *Life* magazine.

Seldom was an act more warmly welcomed.

The Trio, Dennis, Lindsey and Phil.

Gary, however, wasn't happy with the arrangement, and he soon broke away from the group to stake a career in the movies, where he played Elvis Presley's foil on occasion, and television. The other three had new publicity photos taken of them as a trio, and they continued performing. But the group never met with any great success.

As young men will, they married, bought homes, and had children.

Their relationships with women, including their wives, were not lasting ones for the most part, and for any number of the usual reasons. I think Uncle Bing welcomed his daughters-in-law and the expansion of the family and becoming a grandfather. However, as each of his sons divorced, played roundelay with new partners, and had children out of wedlock, Bing seemed to turn his back on them, out of sheer disappointment, I think. Their antics opposed the Catholic principles under which Uncle Bing had been raised, and their conduct violated the standards that he wanted for his family.

Although the Crosby name opened doors for the brothers, they appeared to be unable or unwilling to walk through them. I think they simply didn't have the dedication it takes to craft a successful life.

When Uncle Bing died he left money to his four sons.

Gary received his inheritance right away, according to a biographer, Michael Freedland. It pleased Bing that Gary had stopped drinking, gone into Alcoholics Anonymous, and settled down into a fairly stable married life.

How ironic, then, that Gary would author the book that demonized his father. Shortly before his death from cancer, I talked to Gary about making a recording with his father, the way Natalie Cole did with her dad, Nat, but there wasn't enough time.

Bing with his first four boys

To be fair to them, the boys had lived an unreal life from the very beginning. As children, their time in public was rationed very strictly, a holdover from the hysteria over the Lindbergh kidnapping. When they did venture out, Georgie would explain to them that people wanted to take their picture because they were such nice looking and polite boys. They were never to be told that they were the sons of a celebrity, or anyone special at all. They found that out later.

Lindsay, Phil, Dennis and Gary.

At various times over the years, gossip would fly in the media regarding Uncle Bing's first four boys. This time it was a piece of shocking news, the death of Bing and Dixie's son Dennis, Phillip's twin brother, by his own hand. Some time later, the youngest of the four, Lindsey would also commit suicide. The words "tragic" and "heartbreaking" are hardly strong enough to describe the feeling, the emotional distress that overtook their families.

Rumors were rife at the time that the boys had done the ultimate deed because they were facing financial failure. While it may be hard to believe that any of Bing Crosby's sons would ever be broke, it was difficult as well to understand that even if it were true, how being without funds is a reason to end your life.

I went in search of the truth. I spent several hours interviewing Lindsay's widow, Susan, who was anxious to set things straight. Over a long afternoon, Susan told me about her husband's illness: manic depression, or bipolar. This is a condition whereby an individual experiences extreme "highs" and "lows" of behavior that are uncontrollable, but medication helps.

Susan speaks freely about the years leading up to the loss of her husband. There is no doubt that Linny suffered from a mental illness.

Lindsay, (I always called him "Linny" from the time we were kids), had four children and spent 24 years making a home and a life with his Susan. Whatever demons plagued Dennis, Linny's were different. Always known to be the quietest one of the bunch, I think Uncle Bing somewhat favored him, being the youngest.

Bing and Dixie with baby Lindsay

Bing at son Lindsay's high school graduation

Add to this, the fact that Grandma Kate told Bing to expect great things of Lindsay, because he was the fourth son of a fourth son. I guess that was some Irish belief. But Linny chose a modest life of raising horses and coaching his sons' teams.

He liked to garden and was a big help around the house, pretty much a typical lifestyle, except that this was Los Angeles and it was full of groupies.

Shortly before he died, Lindsay learned that his trust fund income was about to be cut in half. This information tends to cloud the issue of being despondent over money and yet, it clearly must have deepened his depression.

Uncle Bing chose Lindsay to go with him on a trip to Europe, as shown in the following photos. Linny was about 15 years old, he clearly loved traveling with his dad.

Bing and Lindsay in Europe

Bing and Lindsay on the town in Europe

Bing and Lindsay in France

Bing and Lindsay ready for lunch

Bing and Lindsay at an outdoor cafe

Bing and Lindsay in England

Bing and Lindsay are tourists

Bing and Lindsay get the royal treatment

Lindsay's brother Dennis had several children and had been married to Arlene for over 20 years. Many of those years were spent living in Carmel, California, not far from my mother's home. Denny's two daughters were very much a part of his life, he would flash a huge smile and tell me about driving them to their various activities, which he was happy and proud to do. Whether it was to the stables for riding lessons, or to the tennis club, he wanted to be a dad that was involved and close to his girls.

Knowing this about him made his death doubly sad for me. Although we had not spent much time together in our adult years, our visits were always marked by laughter and conversations that had a quality all their own.

I attended Denny's funeral in Los Angeles and sat there in disbelief as my cousins, family friends and other relatives paid their last respects. As the organ music softly played and the altar boys lit the candles, my thoughts went back to the summers of many years ago, to the boy in the swimming pool at the house in Taluca Lake, the kid with the reddish hair and freckled face. I was remembering Dennis the man, at the Crosby Pro-Am in room #123, standing over there by the window in his blue glasses, with his arm around Arlene.

Phillip, Dennis' twin, was the last of Bing and Dixie's four boys to pass away.

He was both married and divorced during his lifetime and I believe he fathered six children.

Although we seldom saw each other in later years, I'll always remember him with curly blonde hair and a really great smile.

Cousin Phil invested in some small businesses and I'm told that he also had an interest in a restaurant, where he would drop in unexpectedly and sing a few songs at the piano. Of all the four boys, Phil seemed the most astute at managing his finances.

He kept to himself for many of his last years, preferring to sleep by day and live by night. His life style was somewhat reclusive, yet the friends he did have spoke warmly of him when I attended his funeral. He died at age sixty nine.

In Loving Memory of
Philip Lang Crosby
Born
July 13, 1934 – Los Angeles, CA
Passed Away
January 13, 004 – Woodland Hills, CA

Funeral Mass
Monday, January 19, 2004 ~ 7:00 pm
Good Shepherd Church
Celebrant
Father Patrick Cahalan, S.J.
Graveside
Tuesday, January 20, 2004 ~ 10:00 am
Holy Cross Cemetery

LORD make me an instrument of Thy peace; where there is hatred, let me sow love; where there is injury, pardon; where there is doubt, faith; where there is despair, hope; where there is darkness, light; and where there is sadness, joy.

7. BUT BEAUTIFUL

I call the Mapleton Drive address a home, but like most properties in the area, it would be more accurately described as a small estate. Six bedrooms in total, carefully-tended gardens, a flagstone driveway which hummed with posh and gleaming cars on social days, an eight-car stable for Uncle Bing's own sedans and, of course, his golf cart.

In addition to Georgie and Louis, there was a full-time cook, Rose and a laundress who came in a couple of times a week. That was the extent of the household staff that "did things for Mr. Crosby."

I was given the guest's quarters, just adjacent to my grandmother's rooms, where she and I would spend a good deal of time visiting together, often watching her favorite television programs, which included baseball games. Anything involving the Pittsburgh Pirates, in which Bing had an interest, was eyed especially keenly.

I said we visited, but that's not entirely accurate. "Visiting" for Grandma Kate usually involved questioning me about the length of my skirt, while peering intently for telltale ear-piercing, which was forbidden. She also would wonder aloud whether I *really* wanted to wear that particular shade of lipstick, while darkly warning me about dating outside the religion and the other sundry perils which might befall a girl in the midst of the big, bad city.

It was no wonder that Grandma Kate had a second nickname: "The Boss."

Uncle Bing and I spent time together, too, when he wasn't traveling on business or flying off to some hunting expedition, personal appearance, or movie location somewhere. I think my timing was lucky. His was an exceptionally busy life, but in the years between Aunt Dixie's death and his marriage to Kathryn Grant in 1957, I suspect he had a need to be close to his family, which had been his anchor from the very beginning. Helping out his sister's daughter was, I believe, fulfilling for him.

Uncle Bing with pipe, what else?

Speaking of filling, a hot and nutritious breakfast fortified each morning. Uncle Bing would offer a hearty, "Come on, Carolyn! Let's go! Seven o'clock!" and he'd whistle his way down that circular staircase and on to the cozy and bright family breakfast room. That whistle is a sound which still comfortably resonates with me, as I know it does with his millions of fans. But to hear it in person, as soundtrack to a bright and shining southern California daybreak. Well, it is difficult to put that kind of thing into words.

The table was set for us and Rose would appear to ask what we might like to have today. Grandma usually had a tray brought to her room. During breakfast, Uncle Bing would read the paper, with appropriate editorial comments, sip his coffee, and we'd converse.

Well, *I'd* converse.

He'd be questioning me about how the Nash sedan he had loaned me was running, what my plans were for the day, whether I had phoned my mother to check in, whether any boys had been bothering me, and, by the way, had I been attending Mass regularly?

I can't say for certain, but he probably also had conspired with his mother in checking the condition of my earlobes.

Uncle Bing had left standing orders long before that there were to be no phone calls at breakfast. He preferred to enjoy it in his usual relaxed and comfortable manner. This telephone embargo lasted from the pouring of the (Minute Maid) orange juice to the climax of the meal, when he would produce his trusty toothpick.

This was the Uncle Bing I knew at Mapleton Drive with pipe and toupee, as usual

Seeing this international star efficiently working his toothpick amused me to no end. Despite the trappings of his success, which were all around me, my uncle tried as diligently as he could to be "just one of the fellas," and it was easy to regard him that way.

Bing at Pebble Beach.

He famously hated his "scalp doily," and onscreen would wear hats whenever he got the chance, to cover his balding scalp. He dressed haphazardly to the point where he was once ejected from a Vancouver hotel for arriving unkempt from a hunting trip. It is hard to understand now, when fame seems to be its own reward, but Uncle Bing never seemed comfortable with celebrity, with being a "big shot."

I certainly had no clue what being a big shot might be like, although I figured I might like to try it on and see if it fit.

Which is not to say I was too naïve to realize that fame carried with it a dark side. No one who read movie magazines as voraciously as I did, and I started early, pawing through Grandpa Harry's extensive collection, could escape the horror stories. Fame carries a heavy price tag.

I became acquainted with some of celebrity's somewhat smaller annoyances during my time at 594 Mapleton Drive.

I recall one day when I chanced to glance outside and spied a middle-aged woman sitting on a bench out in the driveway opening a paper bag, the kind with twine handles that you used to get at the grocery store. She was happily removing its contents, and when she pulled out the Thermos, I quickly understood that this was her lunch and apparently she was preparing to enjoy it right then and there.

Now, what the heck is going on here? I wondered. I called to Georgie. She looked outside and, in a voice that indicated this was hardly something new for her, said, "Awe, my gosh!"

"What's she up to, anyway?" I asked, watching our visitor peeling an orange.

"Well," Georgie sighed, "people hoping to catch a glimpse of your uncle coming and going from the house will just plop themselves right out there in the driveway and sit there for as long as it takes until he comes by."

"So what do you do?"

She regarded our uninvited picnicker for a moment. "You call the police," she said matter-of-factly, picking up the phone, "and they ask her to leave."

As I've noted, it's not as if I didn't harbor a little secret hope that, one day, I might be so famous that people would be coming from all over to have lunch in my driveway. The fame bug had bit me. Hard!

So it was that, shortly after my arrival, I started a job at Paramount Studios that Uncle Bing had arranged for me.

The "Talent Department" was where I was working, or, to be more precise, learning. Along with other aspiring actors and actresses I would attend acting and diction classes and such, in an effort to, as they say, hone my craft.

Members of the department would also show up at premieres and other events around town. Anything to get ourselves noticed.

And, of course, we spent a lot of time hoping. That's why we were called "hopefuls."

I recall a day when one of my fellow hopefuls and I were going to attend a show together. He said he'd stop by to pick me up for the evening and asked where I lived.

It was a revelation how easy the answer came: "I live," I said, "at 594 Mapleton Drive."

It was a revelation to him, too, when he saw the place.

8. SWINGING ON A STAR

Although I had a bit of an "in" at Paramount, I still had to undergo an interview by Mr. Bill Michaeljohn, a burly, businesslike man whom Uncle Bing described as the fellow at the studio who did the hiring and firing.

"But don't worry," Uncle Bing said. "Bill's a good guy. I don't think he'll turn you down, not this soon, anyway."

He was right. Mr. Michaeljohn was a good guy. Our brief meeting couldn't have been more pleasant, although it was difficult for me to sell him on the idea that I was a terrific actress. In my nervousness, I had forgotten Uncle Bing's advice: this was no time to be humble.

Nevertheless, at meeting's end, Mr. Michaeljohn said he was willing to sign me on as a contract player, a term I had up to that point only heard in regard to the game of bridge, and instructed me to make myself available for any kind of acting work at the studio—whether it was on film, performing a voice-over, or, more commonly, rehearsing a scene with an actor or actress preparing for a screen test. When I told Uncle Bing I'd been hired he said, "Don't let me down now, if Paramount thinks I've sent them a lemon, I'll be back working with Hope."

Mr. Michaeljohn also sent me to meet Michael Curtiz, who had directed Uncle Bing's friend Humphrey Bogart in *Casablanca* and had helmed many other blockbusters, including *Life with Father*, *The Adventures of Robin Hood*, and *Yankee Doodle Dandy*. Curtiz had recently finished making *White Christmas* with my uncle and Rosemary Clooney, and I was so thrilled, and so nervous, upon meeting him that I honestly can't remember what the devil he said, nor what the devil I was sent to talk to him about. It's probably just as well.

I was quite conscious that nerve-wracking meet-and-greets like these were being arranged for me by Paramount because Uncle Bing had asked the studio big wigs to do him a favor. Bing was so respected, and so well-liked, which is not always the same thing, that the studio would have done just about anything for him.

Of course, once I was truly "in," Paramount's crack publicity team charged into action, crafting press releases ballyhooing that the "Versatile Niece of Bing Crosby Is at Paramount," as one put it.

They sure did know how to hype a girl:

"Although a good-looking, hazel-eyed, young damsel with dark hair, Carolyn has no desire for the glamour-gal type career, she wants to be a comedienne."

"A graduate of San Jose State College, where she majored in drama and appeared in several plays, Carolyn is the 'Eve Arden' type, quick on the comeback, but possessing a touch of her Uncle Bing's nonchalant humor."

"The field's more wide-open for comediennes and character-type actresses," she explains.

"Carolyn's been known to play everything from the gum-chewing burlesque queen and English maid to the aloof and sophisticated snob. Her audition saw Carolyn throw caution to the winds and get bedecked in a 1941-type dress, a big hat with a tall, straight flower, and an old ivy leaf draped lifelessly at her side, definitely no competition for Marilyn Monroe in the wardrobe department."

The story also quoted me as saying that I wanted an acting part so bad, "I'd even play a corpse on *Dragnet*."

I have to admit that bit of hyperbole was, actually, "the facts ma'm, just the facts".

I had nearly gotten used to living at 594 Mapleton when the Hollywood Studio Club phoned Uncle Bing one day to say they had an opening for me. Though going out on my own away from the sheltering presence of Uncle Bing, and the claustrophobia of Grandma Kate's inquisitions, was an intimidating prospect, I was quite excited about joining the Club.

I packed my things in the good old trusty Samsonite once more and drove into Hollywood, ready to move into my new digs. I had signed up to share a room and was lucky enough to draw a roommate who was a blond singer. She also doubled as a nurse to earn real money, like a lot of the girls did. We became good friends. Most of us at the Club had regular 8 to 5 jobs, while others worked at night. One of the girls, Barbara Huffman, was a line dancer at a famous night club on Sunset Blvd. She really wanted to be an actress, so she hired an agent and changed her name to Barbara Eden. Sound familiar? How about "I Dream of Jeannie?" I found that I really liked living at the Club, uncle Bing had made a good choice for me.

And was it ever convenient!

The Studio Club was within walking distance of a side gate of the studio. It was the beginning of summer, a bright beginning you might say, to a full year of a truly wonderful experience. It was about a twenty minute walk so I wore comfortable shoes and being short funded, carried my own lunch. I never got over the thrill of reporting for work, and sauntering under the big metal arch that read, PARAMOUNT PICTURES.

Bob Hope greeted mother, me (I'm at right), and some of my friends on the set of The Lemon Drop Kid

I'd visited the studio several times in my younger days, once with mother and some friends to say hello to Bob Hope on the set of one of his pictures, *The Lemon Drop Kid*. True-to-form when he had an audience of any size at all, Bob delivered an impromptu monologue for us. Uncle Bing once said Hope loved performing so much he'd do 20 minutes at a bus stop.

So I was familiar with the layout, but going there to work was an entirely different thing. Even so, I quickly felt a part of the place. I had a one-year contract at Paramount and I was going to make the most of it. I was going to savor every minute of every single day.

When we arrived each morning at the Talent Department, Katie, the delightful little Munchkin-like woman who pretty much ran the place, would hand the other players and me our mimeographed schedule.

Our workroom was called "The Goldfish Bowl", for good reason. It was a bedroom-sized area with three ordinary walls and a glass "observation wall." Charlotte Clary, our director, would sit in one of the theater seats on the other side of the glass, watch us perform, and give us her occasionally withering critique. If we needed a little help with our diction, we were told to counsel with Mr. Luther, our in-house coach.

Sometimes, Charlotte would give us scripts to study at home, a scene or two from a play or a movie. We would perform them for her in the Goldfish Bowl the following day. We also did a lot of improvisation to hone our skills for what we all dreamed would be our nothing short of sensational future in the movies.

Katie told us one morning that a young German actress would be coming in to work with Mr. Luther. She was being considered by Paramount for a couple of roles, but her accent was deemed too thick for the American market.

Mr. Luther's mission was to "flatten her out a bit."

One look at the new girl and you knew that flattening her would require some sort of steam press. Her other attributes included a pleasant enough manner, although she was a little bit shy and reluctant to engage in conversation, likely self-conscious about her accent.

When we weren't on call, we were encouraged to visit any of the sets that were active and filming, to "enhance our experience." The day the new girl arrived, Uncle Bing was working with Donald O'Connor on Stage Four, doing Cole Porter's *Anything Goes*, and I decided to drop by.

When the director called for lunch, Uncle Bing asked me to break bread with him in his "dressing room", a bungalow which could have doubled as a pretty nice little home. We ate and chatted, interrupted by a constant stream of the usual visitors, wardrobe people, gag writers, publicists.

In the course of our talk, Uncle Bing asked me what I was going to do later that afternoon, and I said, "Cecil B. DeMille is on the set today, filming *The Ten Commandments*. I have to go watch that!"

Uncle Bing agreed that might definitely "enhance my experience."

I also mentioned the new German girl that we had met that morning. "Oh really?" he said. "a new Fraulein on the lot, "what's her name?"

I told him it was a funny one. "Ursula Andress."

On the set at Paramount with Uncle Bing with Tallulah Bankhead and assorted Hollywood types. I'm seated at the upper center of the photo, in the midst of the whirl.

He agreed that would look pretty unique on a marquee.

When Ursula finally made it big, she made it really big, and not for Paramount, either. Few moviegoers could forget her strolling out of the ocean in a bikini for a very impressed Sean Connery in the first James Bond movie, *Dr. No*.

And Mr. Luther had *nothing* to do with it.

Over the next few months, I happily settled into my routine at the studio. I began to make friends and became a familiar face around the lot. The guard would say a bright "Good morning!" and call me by name when I strolled through the gate. It was still a dream, just a little more familiar dream.

Speaking of dreams, when the 1955 Academy Awards rolled around, I just *had* to go. No two ways about it.

I phoned Uncle Bing to see if he could get tickets for me, nervously hoping that I wasn't imposing too much. These were, after all, not movie passes I was asking for, but literally the hottest tickets in Hollywood.

To my considerable relief, it turned out Uncle Bing was happy I wanted to attend. He felt the event would keep me inspired about pursuing my career. A pair of tickets was promptly mailed to me at the Studio Club.

I needed a date, of course. Luckily, I had befriended a comic I met while I was doing a Red Cross benefit show a few months earlier, and I asked him to be my escort.

He accepted, and said he could borrow his father's Cadillac for the occasion. Another blessing was that he owned a tuxedo. We were going to look smashing, just like everyone else.

And he came with transportation, what a bonus in a young man.

Now, I needed a dress.

I was frantic.

While I'll admit the problem of obtaining a nice dress to wear to the Oscars is an enviable quandary, it is downright harrowing when you're on a budget tighter than Scarlet O'Hara's corset.

Suddenly, I remembered.

Or thought I did. Had I brought it? I rummaged through my closet. Yes.

The prom dress that Aunt Dixie had given me.

I slid it out of the dry cleaners' bag. It still looked good.

It looked great, actually. And I was now living in a town where strapless scandalized exactly nobody.

The Academy Awards were held that year at the Pantages Theater, and emceed by Bob Hope, of course. It is nearly impossible to describe the excitement of driving down Hollywood Boulevard, past Vine Street, to the big searchlights and screaming fans.

Wow! Look at me! I'm going to the Academy Awards! I thought. I couldn't have shouted it, or even whispered it. I was almost breathless.

As the car drew closer to the entrance of the Pantages, I stared in pure awe at the red carpet, and then quickly closed my eyes against the flashbulbs going off.

Celebrities arrived and were welcomed like royalty, which they were, of a sort. Women were still allowed to wear furs in those days and the stars wore them with style. Everyone arriving in formal wear gave the occasion a regal appearance.

The crowd of onlookers was held in restraint by a thick velvet rope, but some of the teenagers had managed to sneak through the barrier to get a closer look at the storied arrivals when the parking attendant opened their doors.

I had my window rolled down, and one of the young girls poked her head in the car, looked at my date, looked at me, and then turned to her friends in back of her and said, "Oh, it's nobody."

Thanks for that dose of reality on my big night, dearie.

While I knew I wasn't exactly *nobody*, I did realize I wasn't precisely well-known yet. But the Paramount publicity guys were working on it.

One afternoon, Katie told me the studio wanted to have some publicity photos taken of me the following day, so when I came in, I should go directly to the make-up department.

A thrill of fear raced through me. I dreaded having still shots taken, because I knew I did not photograph well just sitting there.

But, of course, I did it anyway. That was a direct order.

And I must modestly admit the make-up man did a terrific job.

I was finished with the shoot and walking down the studio's main street, heading back to the Goldfish Bowl, when a man called out to me.

Glamour Girl me. Donna Reed, eat your heart out

He yelled, "Hey! Hello!" He was a couple of blocks from me, but I was quite certain I wouldn't recognize him at any distance. When he drew closer, and I still had no idea who he was, he said, "Aren't you going to say 'Hello'?"

I just stared.

He did too. Then he suddenly apologized. "I'm sorry," he said. "I thought you were Donna Reed!"

I told you that make-up guy was good.

9. WHAT'S NEW

While Paramount was my day-to-day gig, I also spent quite a bit of time amidst the whirring of the Crosby business machine, an industry unto itself.

Crosby, Inc., the office.

Everything Bing.

The Crosby Building was deep in the heart of Hollywood at 9028 Sunset Boulevard. A classic California deco, Uncle Bing called it "a four-story stucco job", the structure was white with blue accents and windows that, when I visited there as a child under the watchful eye of Grandpa Harry, had looked to me like portholes on a ship.

To my adult eyes, they still looked like portholes. It was a building with nautical flair, which properly reflected the breeziness of its namesake and benefactor.

The boulevard itself was a bustling and colorful street, as alive as any thoroughfare anywhere has ever been and the traffic was terrific. Here were restaurants and bars; there were dress shops, exclusive men's stores and florists. Huge billboards for the movies of the day loomed down on men in linen, gaberdene and sharkskin suits, accompanied often by women attired in cotton, silk and voile, their outfits topped off by some sort of elaborate hat. It was a fast-moving street as well, everybody gave the impression of being on some urgent mission, even if it was just a trek to obtain a martini or two at the Mocambo or Ciro's, or Scandia, which was a favorite restaurant of the Crosby men.

It could be said, in fact, that the Crosby men put Scandia on the Hollywood map. It was, as its name implies, one of those Nordic places, and its patrons actually occasionally sported horned Viking helmets after they'd consumed a ration or two or three of their favorite grog. It was fun, in other words, and owner Kenneth Hansen appreciated my uncles' business so much he coronated them among the first of his "Viking Chiefs", a title they regarded as a real honor. And as a "Chief", each uncle was given a stein with his name on it, which hung in the back bar, awaiting his use. Scandia also was a generous place, doing its considerable bit for the local charities, which greatly pleased its regulars from down the street.

You would often see Sunset Boulevard regulars dining al fresco, silverware gleaming and clinking in what seemed the ever-present sun of those days. At the curb, long black limos parked and flashed their chrome, their chauffeurs standing in alert readiness for their bosses, sometimes rather uncomfortably clutching a wiggling poodle which wanted desperately to chase "Madam" into the hairdresser.

Or into the Crosby Building that was Uncle Everett's bailiwick.

Uncle Ev ran the place in tandem with my Uncle Larry. My Uncle Ted was quite a businessman as well, but after helping Bing with his acquisition of the Del Mar race track in 1937, he had returned to Washington state, where he enjoyed a long and very successful career with Washington Water and Power.

Grandpa Harry also worked in the Crosby Building. I say "worked" and he did perform some various labors, but grandpa's position was also created as a convenient method of getting him away from home for a few hours, particularly when Grandma Kate was being a little uppity. Grandpa's office was at the end of the hall and had a nice oak roll top desk. Other than a dial phone, family pictures on the wall and a big comfortable chair, there wasn't much else to it. I suspect that chair had been the site of many a nap for Grandpa.

Uncle Larry's office room on the other hand, was strictly business. Green metal filing cabinets lined the walls, his desk was piled high with papers, folders, books and photos. Definitively a hard hat working area with no frills, just the opposite of Uncle Ev's office. Uncle Larry would never spend money on antique office furniture the way Uncle Ev did, he was tighter than a rubber band.

In addition to serving as Uncle Bing's manager, Uncle Ev was the family's representative to the wide world of culture. A veteran of the Allied Expeditionary Force stationed in France during World War I, Everett brought back with him knowledge of the European Way that immediately elevated him from his former status as just a kid with ideas from Washington State. He grew to favor the finer things, purchasing expensive furniture and art and in that respect, it was a very good thing that Uncle Ev knew how to make money, big piles of it.

He lived in a grand home on Bellagio Road with his second wife, Florence, whom I presume you might have guessed was an opera singer. She even occasionally wangled a spot on Bing's radio show.

Imagine that.

Uncle Everett, right, during World War I.

Everett's place was the scene of elaborate, formal, dinners followed by far less formal drinks in "The Playroom," which is what he called his bar. This particular playroom stocked some pretty good stuff. Mother recalled an occasion when a partygoer ordered up a Scotch and Everett popped downstairs to the cellar and emerged again to pour him a libation from a pre-World War I bottle of Haig and Haig, talk about smooth! Uncle Ev was an imposing man. Everything about him was big, from the cufflinks he wore to the deals he made. Flamboyant, well-dressed to the point of overdressing, on occasion sporting a carefully-tended Mischa Auer type moustache, Everett Crosby was the sort of man who had an aviary built where beautiful, tropical birds fluttered and sang. He was also the sort of man who took pride in putting a caged monkey on his patio.

We all hated that monkey.

But meanwhile back at the office.

You passed into Uncle Ev's domain through huge, imposing, double doors, where he held court behind an oaken desk, often smoking a fat cigar from his humidor, and looking pretty much like God there at the end of the room. That is, if God was a size "portly."

Bing and Everett both enjoyed a knack for business, but Everett was the one who got the deals done. Still, while Uncle Ev's instincts were usually quite good, there were some days when the gray cells weren't, to mix the metaphors, firing on all cylinders.

On one of those occasions, a man strolled into Uncle Ev's office with what he thought was a surefire notion. "This television thing is going to be quite the medium," the man said.

"Yes," Uncle Ev muttered, somewhat less than enthusiastically. "Bing might try a little something on television. We've talked about it."

"I was thinking that a Western, a cowboy thing, might really go over well, something for kids."

Uncle Ev and his visitor tossed around the notion for awhile, but Everett in the end was unimpressed. "I think you'd better try someplace else. I don't think it's going to work. Sorry."

The visitor shrugged, shook hands warmly with Uncle Ev, and asked that his regards be delivered to Bing.

Then William Boyd, Hoppalong Cassidy, exited the office and galloped right smack dab into television history, for another agent. Uncle Bing ribbed his brother about that for years.

If Uncle Ev wasn't entirely perfect, he sure was good enough to steer Uncle Bing to quality projects, and he had done so right from the beginning of their business relationship. He was, in fact, living in Los Angeles and working as a talent scout, theatrical agent and bootlegger's assistant before Bing decided to take his own crack at the city in 1928. Everett recalled that, when Bing asked if he could stay with him until he found a singing job, "I figured I could sing better than he could, but I said, 'If you're going to live with me, you're going to work."

In later years, Bing would make it a running gag on his radio show that Everett was the laziest of the Crosby brothers. That was exactly backwards, of course, and off the radio, Bing always credited Uncle Ev with providing the get-up-and-go he lacked. Without Everett, Bing's career-making, record-breaking, appearance of 29 weeks at the Paramount Theater in New York would not have happened, and he may never have inked his contract with CBS, one of the richest and longest-lived pacts in the history of radio. Uncle Ev even helped finagle his brother his first "A-picture" appearance, in *The Big Broadcast of 1932*. Uncle Ev was responsible for creating, from the raw material of his talented brother, one of the brightest stars in show business.

As top banana at Bing Crosby Enterprises, second only to Bing himself, Everett's first priority was show biz, but he also represented other artists over the years, everyone from Robert Preston to Daryl Hickman.

In tandem with Uncle Larry, who handled Crosby-related publicity (including bailing out Bing's boys on occasion and hushing up the story) Uncle Ev kept on the constant lookout for new business ventures for Bing, which ranged from the sublime, Minute Maid Orange Juice springs to mind for some reason, to the mildly ridiculous and forgettable Bing Crosby Ice Cream.

Bing Crosby Ice Cream. Not the best idea ever

The brothers also were tasked with locating the Next Big Things, those inventions that would set the world aflame, and to that end they founded Crosby Research, with Larry at the helm.

Uncle Everett tries to convince Aunt Kay, Grandma Kate, and Everett's wife, Florence, that some sort of Crosby Research gizmo will change their lives for the better, Grandma looks decidedly unimpressed

Mother and I were quite familiar with the activities of Crosby Research, because we were among its guinea pigs. Samples of some pretty crazy inventions were sent to us for a test run.

Packages frequently would arrive at our home up north in Alameda, bearing the address of the Crosby office. Inside would be some contraption or other which usually carried no indication of its purpose or operation.

One such item was a motion detector. This little gem was to be connected to your living room lamp. It was meant to be a security device, if an intruder entered your home, the lamp would flicker. The only problem was you would have to be in the house to see the light go off and on. Doesn't that sort of defeat the purpose? I think someone in the planning department got fired over that one.

Next on the list were the toilet paper dispensers. This invention was created to cut down on excessive use of paper and reduce expenses. A person would be limited to only a few sheets at a time. Some of them were actually sold, to Los Angeles County offices, for their workers. Not a hot seller, Crosby Research became overstocked, so Uncle Larry took them home and put them in his garage to be given out later as Christmas gifts. When Aunt Kay received one, she was not amused.

During the war years, in the 1940's, some inventor came to Crosby Research with one of the most laughable ideas to walk through the door. It was a camouflage make-up kit, intended for home use. I guess if you wanted to be the first one on your block to look like a bush, or if you needed a disguise for your next spy mission, this creation was just the ticket. The few prototypes that were made also ended up on Larry's gift list.

On a more serious note, Crosby Research engaged in many worthwhile ventures such as the manufacture of airplane parts for the military and was responsible for the development of the tape recorder as well as several other valuable projects.

Uncle Larry was also a great believer in recycling, even before it became mandatory. He was especially interested in anything that was free of charge and could be passed around in the family. He was a benevolent "giver" and he found great joy and pleasure in not letting anything go to waste. For many years it was his habit to stop by at Bing's house once a week to visit and discuss business matters. At that time, if Uncle Bing was disposing of any clothing or housewares, Georgie would give them to Uncle Larry. Delighted with his new found treasures, Larry would set about dispensing them like some kind of Robin Hood. Family members were on the receiving end of things like blazer jackets, shoes, Dixie's handbags and such. On one occasion, there was a pair of Bing's shoes that he had used in a movie. Not being a very tall man, sometimes the wardrobe department would put lifts in the shoes, these were called "elevators". Uncle Larry gave them to his son Jack, who sat down to try them on and see how they fit. When poor Jack stood up, not knowing they were the "elevators" he pitched forward and almost fell flat on his face.

After he felt enough time had passed for us to fully appreciate whatever gadget he had sent our way, Uncle Larry would phone to inquire if we liked the whatchamacallit, and whether the Crosby Research Institute should invest in it.

Now, while a research department sounds like one of those pie-in-the-sky activities men get around to when they have way too much money and free time and it certainly was. One of its projects would radically alter show business, and just about every other business everywhere and all because Uncle Bing wanted to carve out a little more of that free time he prized.

I heard that it was shortly after World War II when a man named John Mullin showed up at the Crosby Building with a unique invention. It used magnetic tape to very accurately record sound, and Mullin said that when it was demonstrated for him in Germany he really flipped.

Der Bingle had the same reaction.

Mullin recalled that Uncle Bing told him he resented the regimentation imposed by live radio broadcasts. Some weeks he wasn't in the mood and hated doing a broadcast. At other times he was ready to do two or three at a crack. He didn't like having to keep an eye on the clock and being directed to speed things up or draw them out. Besides, he got to the point where he really didn't like having to do two "live" shows, one for the east coast and three hours later, one for the west coast.

Uncle Bing, with one of the first tape recorders

The brothers Crosby instantly saw the tape recorder's potential. Uncle Bing realized that not only would the machine make it possible for him to record his programs free of the tyranny of live broadcasting, it would also make editing them a snap. He could do 45 minutes or even an hour, remove the extraneous material, the jokes and songs that didn't work, and after editing, have a half-hour program as close to perfect as it could be. In association with the Ampex Company, Uncle Bing provided the wherewithal, the influence, and the enthusiasm needed to develop the tape recorder for commercial use. He also waged a prolonged battle against those entrenched entertainment executives who argued that tape recording would never be practical. In the end, Uncle Bing won the day, and the rest is recorded history.

I discovered to my delight that the fascination I felt for the Crosby Building as a child of ten, when it was a real thrill just to be able to use the water cooler whenever I wanted, hadn't dimmed a bit now that I was there as an adult. You might think that a young girl wouldn't be interested in such a place, but the Crosby offices on Sunset Blvd. were definitely out of the ordinary. I still marveled at all the action, it was a beehive of activity, just as I had remembered. The adventure began as soon as I walked in the door, the receptionist greeted me and I wandered from room to room. I had free rein of the place, but spent most of my time in the mail room because it was the most lively. In one part, women were seated at long tables scanning through piles of newspapers and magazines, particularly copies of the trade papers, *Hollywood Reporter* and *Variety*, clipping every mention of Bing. In another part, a whole retinue of young women were sliding requested autographed eight-by-ten glossy photographs of my uncle into manila envelopes.

I watched in pure amazement as three or four of the office girls sorted the hundreds of fan letters, which came in by the bagful daily, quite often bearing colorful stamps from countries all around the world. I could have stayed there all day.

Here in this busy building, perhaps more than anywhere else, I began to understand what a global franchise just being Bing Crosby had become.

JUST BING

Uncle Bing gets ready to let it rip

10. STRAIGHT DOWN THE MIDDLE

But enough of business, after spending so much time at the office, Uncle Bing would insist that it's time we break for a round of golf, or two.

My uncle's famous preoccupation with the game lasted exactly as long as he did. He told anyone who would listen that the time he spent on courses throughout the world calmed and centered him, that his stresses appeared to evaporate like the morning dew off the fairway when he stepped up to the first tee.

His dedication to the game was unsurpassed, and had its fondest expression in "The Clambake", the Bing Crosby Pro-Am golf tournament at Pebble Beach.

Even a girl like me who was not particularly interested in sports could hardly help but notice there was something special going on out there in Monterey, on the California coast.

Attracting the brightest names in both golf and show business, Uncle Bing's tournament annually provided an easy mix of serious competition on the course, paired with elaborate tomfoolery in the clubhouse and at after-hours parties. It was a combination that quickly won the hearts of golfers and golf fans everywhere. Especially at Club Nineteen, that's where golfers go after the 18th hole, to compare their scorecards and order up a booze burger.

While I was busy emoting at San Jose State College, my mother purchased a home in Carmel, California. I thought it was beautiful and very pricey for its time. It surely was the best house she had ever owned. Ecstatic about her new residence, mother was also pleased that Uncle Bing's annual Pro-Am was headquartered just a few miles away.

She phoned me at school one evening and invited me down for the tournament weekend to take it all in. "It'll be fun," she said.

What a gift she had for understatement!

"The Crosby", as it was referred to by just about everybody, was nothing *but* fun, each and every year it was played. Not just another pretty face on the PGA Tour, it was the quintessential pro-am, and it had Uncle Bing's demeanor all over it.

My links-crazy uncle had hosted his National Pro-Am at Rancho Santa Fe, in southern California, for six years, beginning in 1937, before putting it on hiatus for the duration of World War II. After hostilities calmed, a sportswriter named Ted Durein wired the Crosby Building and suggested the tournament be moved north, to Pebble Beach, where Bing had a home. Crosby, Inc. thought it an interesting idea and Uncle Larry was dispatched to negotiate the terms.

So it was that "The Crosby" came to "The Peninsula" in 1947 and was to be held there every year in January.

Located on the windswept northern California coast, the scenic beauty of the area had long been noted by travelers, poets, artists and crooners, for that matter. With a backdrop of pines and cypress, and a magnificent view of the Pacific, Pebble Beach proved an outstanding venue for the sport. It was there that a mix of tour pros, show business celebrities, and unpredictable, sometimes god-awful— weather combined to produce a legend of the Grand Old Game, where camaraderie and humor were nearly as important as sportsmanship.

Popular logo used all through the Tournament years.

Uncle Bing's Pebble Beach home overlooked the golf course.

In that regard, my Uncle Bob was the unfortunate subject of a tale many a duffer will relate to, but which ultimately serves as an example of just how important sportsmanship was to Bing.

Invited to play in the Pro-Am one year, Bob had a terrible round—so bad in fact, that he got angry with himself, Pebble Beach, and the Pacific Ocean where he launched his clubs upon completion of his ordeal.

Family loyalty aside, when Bing caught wind of Bob's tantrum that was it. He never invited his younger brother to compete in the tournament again. Not that Bob would have wanted to.

"Don't give up your Bobcats," Bing further advised him, referring to Bob's band.

Disastrous rounds weren't rare at the Crosby. The weather I referred to earlier was often the cause of serious misfortune for the frequently windblown and rain-pelted golfers.

But the ultimate natural insult was probably the snow that covered the fairways during the 1962 renewal of the tournament.

One of my favorite golfers, Jimmy Demeret, who was renowned for his colorful costumes and equally colorful play both on and off the course, famously observed that, "I know I got loaded last night, but how did I end up in Squaw Valley?" (a popular ski resort). Loaded or not, Jimmy was always popular with the gallery of golfing fans that lined the courses at Cypress, Spyglass and Pebble Beach. They could hardly wait to see him every day. His splashy outfits were a thing of legend. On any given day, he could be seen on the course dressed in something like a bright pink sweater over purple plus fours, with argyle socks and a snazzy pair of two tone wing tip golf shoes. What a picture.

The Pebble Beach Lodge is the scene of most of my own memories of Uncle Bing's tournament. My not being a golfer has a little something to do with that.

Of course, I did occasionally go out on the course to watch the competition, but during those early years, there was no seating area for spectators, so following the action meant you had to be just plain nuts about golf, pretty darned athletic and, perhaps most importantly, have in your possession one of those portable stools to occasionally hunker down on. This being Pebble Beach, you also were best advised to keep your rain gear at hand. And it's a good thing too, because one year when my cousin Howard Crosby was playing in the tournament, he bent over to tee up his ball and split the back side of his trousers wide open. Luckily he had a pair of solid color rain togs in his golf bag. Talk about embarrassing moments, Howard made the gossip columns by the seat of his pants.

Eventually, Uncle Bing bowed to popular demand and arranged for bleachers to be erected around the 18th green to accommodate the crowd, which allowed the spectators to enjoy the players' final approaches and putts in comfort.

I was taking advantage of the bleacher seating one year in the mid 1970's when I looked around to see who was watching the action with me. Five feet away sat Betty Ford, intently eyeing her husband, former president Gerald Ford, as he finished up his round. How thrilled I was to be in such auspicious company for the weekend. But, then, auspicious company was part of the package. Mrs. Ford looked lovely. She had a beautiful complexion as I remember and a warm smile, probably because her hubby didn't lob a golf ball into the crowd that year.

President Gerald Ford and Mary Rose

Situated just off that 18th green, the lodge struck me right away as a very posh, very old, very golf, very British place. A two-story addition had been appended to the structure, a block of rooms arrayed in a sort of motel style. I thought the add-on was a real step down, because it wasn't at all in keeping architecturally with the main facility, but nevertheless, that was where Uncle Larry had a suite that became a golf tradition. It was, musically enough, room number 123, the first door along the walkway that led from the lodge. I think the golfers would call it a dogleg to the right.

On the heels of the successful negotiations that brought the pro-am north, Bing tapped Uncle Larry to manage the multitude of things the tournament always entailed. This being the Crosby and all, one of the most important items on Larry's agenda was maintaining Room 123 as a hospitality suite for tournament guests.

Program cover for one of Uncle Bing's Pebble Beach tourneys

Enlisting Larry into the cause was an easy call for Bing. Larry had, after all, directed the early tournaments at Rancho Santa Fe, and he was the family expert at public relations, which was always a big part of "The Clambake."

Uncle Larry was an extraordinarily competent man, nearly as important to Bing Crosby's career as his more flamboyant brother, Everett. When he focused his attention and his steel-rimmed glasses on something, it got done. He was totally devoted to Uncle Bing and protected him from every possible harm. Anyone who crossed the line had Larry to deal with.

He was also a bit of a fuddy-duddy, the kind of fellow whose ties were always the height of fashion 20 years before and were often replete with a soup stain from some long-ago luncheon. Uncle Larry was blissfully unaware of little things like that.

Accompanying his ties were suits of equal vintage. As they say, he got a whole lot of wear out of them.

To complete his ensemble, Larry sometimes sported those two-toned shoes with the perforated instep that were fashionable back in the 1920s, which was a cue for smart-aleck family members like me to remind him that the Coolidge Administration had come and gone.

We kidded Uncle Larry, but we always dearly loved him. He was a thoughtful man, very caring about us Crosby youngsters, but my goodness was he tight with a buck, especially when it was Bing's money. In this case his penny pinching ways must have saved Uncle Bing millions over the years. He had access to every single free promotional product in the Crosby closet, and found great personal utility in every one of them—frequently offering them as gifts, even to members of the family.

He was the perfect choice for tournament director. His gentle, self-effacing manner won him hundreds of friends over the years on the Monterey Peninsula.

Bing, Ben Hogan, and Uncle Larry

Uncle Larry knew that he would be out and about for most of the tournament, involved in checking scores, talking to the press and troubleshooting one thing or another, so he delegated authority, asking my mother to serve as hostess in Room 123. Some years his wife, my aunt Elaine would accompany him, but not on a regular basis. I think she preferred to stay at home with her card playing lady friends. And if you're ready for another family nickname, Larry called her "White Feather." Mother said that as newlyweds, Elaine returned from a matinee all ga-ga over an Indian princess in the film by that name. She mentioned it so often that Larry finally used it as an affectionate pet name for her.

Well, of course, mother was delighted at the rare opportunity to become the party queen of the Peninsula, and she slipped into full hostess mode, immediately seeking the assistance of our cousin, Brent Crosby, who lived about 60 miles away.

Brent knew a thing or two about throwing a party. Hoisting a glass, he would intone his signature line, "This is my first drink today . . . In my left hand".

The left-hander's expertise secured, the Crosby-packed shindig was on. Brent arrived at mother's house with smoked turkey and all the accoutrements, including the best rye bread I've ever tasted. After a night of preparation and a quick breakfast the next morning, we converted the kitchen to a picnic production factory—wicker baskets were everywhere, as were coolers and Thermoses and the stuff to put in them.

Then there was the "booze box", a very popular item, containing enormous quantities of bourbon, scotch, gin, vodka and our old standby Olympia Beer by the case, courtesy of Grandpa Harry's former employer.

Everything was then packed up and transported to Room 123, ready for the "Clambake."

The stage was always set by 11 a.m. on the first day of the tournament, when guests began to arrive to chat, eat and drink. Mother was seldom able to venture down on the golf course to see what was actually happening, but ABC had full coverage, with big TV towers placed along the fairways, so the action could be monitored in the hospitality suite by those of us whose "chipping" amounted to the consumption of snack foods.

Uncle Bing would drop by Room 123 several times a day, and his visits were always crowd-pleasers. He'd pop in and say something like, "Holy mackerel! No wonder there's nobody out on the course! Everybody's in here! I don't suppose you have a spare sandwich lying around?"

Bing's son Dennis and his wife were regulars over the years, as was my cousin, Howard Crosby. Bing's other sister—my Aunt Kay—and her daughter Marilyn were also Room 123 regulars.

Arlene and Dennis Crosby

Mary Rose and James Garner

But the men of the hour were the golfers, pro and amateur, and some of the biggest names in the sport paid us a visit. Duffing celebrities like Jack Lemmon, Danny Kaye, Andy Williams, James Garner, Pat Boone, and many, many more also made the scene.

You just never knew who might be walking—or in Phil Harris's case, stumbling—through the door of Party Headquarters.

Dennis Crosby, Mary Rose and Phil Harris

Harris was responsible for one of many observations which became part of Crosby lore, the year he and his partner shockingly won the amateur portion of the tournament.

The hard-partying Harris gazed at the trophy a moment and said, "Man, ain't *this* a blow to clean livin'!" Phil was the only golfer I ever saw pull a full glass of whiskey out of his golf bag while out on the course and never spill a drop. I think Jim Beam was his patron saint.

The hospitality suite resonated with that sort of witty dialogue, accompanied by peals of appreciative laughter. Over the years, greats like Ben Hogan, Sam Snead, Arnold Palmer, Jack Nicklaus, Johnny Miller and other legends of the game would trade stories and good-natured needling there, and they were always very proficient, sometimes withering, when they kidded one another about their game.

Arnold Palmer and Mary Rose

Late each afternoon, 4 or 5 o'clock, Uncle Larry would take a breather, and finally enjoy some of the fun he was working so hard to cultivate. He would announce that he was holding a contest for the best joke of the day, and the winner would receive a stunning prize from his collection of free Crosby merchandise. The ground rules were these: the story had to be quite funny and worth the time it took to tell it, and its success would be based on audience reaction.

Somehow, I won the contest every year. I think Uncle Larry, being my godfather, had just a little something to do with that. My collection of items from the Crosby Research and Crosby Enterprises runneth over.

*Mr. Bing Crosby
cordially invites you to attend a
Cocktail Party
Thursday evening
the twentieth of January
from six-thirty to eight-thirty
Del Monte Hyatt House
One Old Golf Course Road
Monterey, California*

Invitation to one of the Tournament Cocktail parties

The Bing Crosby Pro-Am was a stellar stop for more than 30 years on the PGA tour and annually raised thousands of dollars for any number of charities including the Boys and Girls Clubs of America. By the late 1960s, it had become the most popular televised event on the tour, with Uncle Bing often providing color commentary for the broadcast.

Living room of Bing's Pebble Beach house

While golfers from all over the world hoped to participate in "The Clambake," you teed off there by invitation only. The list of competitors was hand-picked by Mr. Crosby himself.

For several years, Uncle Bing hosted parties and entertained golfers at his home at Pebble Beach, making it sort of the hub of after-hours operations during the tournament. Aunt Dixie had truly loved their Peninsula home, and in her grief over her death, five years after the tournament had begun there, Bing sent Uncle Larry up the coast to the house, to remove all remembrances of her—photos, monogrammed towels, sheets and table linens, the works.

Bing and Dixie's house at Pebble Beach

Bing at the Pebble Beach House

The Pebble Beach house lent itself well to get-togethers all year round, but especially during the tournament. It had a spacious entryway, which opened onto a very comfortable living room. Curved windows looked out over the golf course and the ocean beyond. As a visitor continued into the house, he would find himself in Bing's den, which boasted recording equipment, a selection of pipes for every occasion, framed photographs, and enough office bric-a-brac to let it be known that business was conducted there. A built-in wet bar indicated it wasn't *all* business.

I was saddened to hear that Uncle Bing eventually sold the house, but I certainly understood. The reminders of his years with Dixie may have been excised, but there was no way to erase the memories of the times they had enjoyed in that place. Aunt Dixie told me once that one of her very favorite pleasures had been relaxing in the bathtub there, next to a huge window which allowed her to gaze out past the 13th green and watch the ocean thundering on the rocks.

Bing and Dixie's bedroom in the Pebble Beach house.
Portrait of son Lindsay hangs on right wall

Now that his Pebble Beach property was no longer available at tournament time, Uncle Bing would bed down at the Lodge, or a country club, or with friends. In a few years his young son Nathaniel would become well known and well respected as a amateur golfer. He would spend a couple of nights at my mother's house, his Aunt Mary Rose and practice his putts down her carpeted hallway.

Whether the venue was his home or some other location around town, Bing made certain every year that mother and I were invited to all of the social events that took place in the evenings, and they were fabulous. Cocktail parties, sometimes at the lodge, sometimes at Bing's residence or other private homes, were all about gourmet *hors d'oeuvres* and carved ice sculptures. The conversation was warm, the music cool, and everyone seemed as happy and relaxed as a Crosby aria.

Alice Faye and Mary Rose

Glen Campbell and Mary Rose

I became an item in James Bacon's gossip column as a result of one of these soirees. Bacon wrote that, "Carolyn, daughter of Mary Rose, is the Henny Youngman (a well-known comic of years ago) in the Crosby clan. The family would like to see the attractive Carolyn land a husband."

Bacon noted that Alan Fisher, Bing's butler, made a suggestion which Bacon was able to use for my benefit when I was dining with a particularly handsome young amateur golfer.

The columnist said he took the golfer aside and told him, "Carolyn, you know, is Bing's favorite niece, and she's in his will for $7 million."

"It caught the golfer's immediate attention," the columnist wrote.

TELEGRAMS - "ANCIENT"
TELEPHONE NOS 2112 & 2113
CODE · BENTLEY'S
SECRETARY
K. R. T. MACKENZIE, M.C.
DEPUTY SECRETARY
W. N. B. LOUDON

ROYAL AND ANCIENT GOLF CLUB
OF ST. ANDREWS,
FIFE.

14th March 1977

Dear Mary Rose,

    I am now just putting together all the bits after my most memorable trip to the "Bing Crosby" Tournament, and I could not complete this without writing to thank you for all the kindness you extended to me during my stay at Pebble Beach, both in your private room at the Lodge and at your home on that rather alcoholic evening on the Saturday after we had all failed to qualify for the final day.

    The experience of my trip will remain with me for ever, and perhaps some day I may get the chance again. I am still dining out regularly on the tales I have to tell!

    It was my particular pleasure to meet the "Crosby" family and relations, although understandably I saw little of Bing himself. This is a matter which can be put right on a more private occasion in U.K.

    If you are over here, please get in touch as I would love to see you again.

    Please give my best regards to all whom I met in your company.

Sincerely,
George Wilson

Letter of gratitude from Mr. George Wilson, member,
Royal and Ancient Golf Club of St. Andrews, Scotland.

11. I'LL BE SEEING YOU

When she wasn't acting as a tournament hostess, my mother, my biggest fan, was sort of an ad hoc agent for me, always supportive of my career goals and never averse to helping them along.

Mother phoned me every week to hear about my Hollywood adventures, and to encourage me. Her brother, my Uncle Bob Crosby, hosted a daily network TV show at the time, a musical and variety program for CBS that was broadcast live at noon each day, Monday through Friday,

Mother asked me if I wanted to appear on the show, and if it would help me to get ahead in show business.

"Well, it surely couldn't hurt", I told her.

Uncle Bob's program was quite popular, particularly among those housewives who were home to see it. Hence its theme song: "Housewives Serenade." It ran from 1952 to 1956 and featured Bob's band, the Bobcats, along with an enthusiastic group of regulars, and the occasional special guest.

"I'd love to do it," I said, "but he hasn't asked me."

"Well," mother replied, "I'll talk to him."

Sure enough, a few days later, I received a call from CBS inviting me to appear on *The Bob Crosby Show*. Even though it was "all in the family," and I would be in a supportive environment there on the set, the butterflies took wing once again.

I was invited to meet with the show's staff to formulate some sort of skit, and it was decided the segment would be a singing duet spiced with comedy.

The writers asked me, "What exactly do you do?"

I said I preferred to do comedy, but I could carry a tune if it wasn't some sort of soaring ballad.

"Well, we'll call you," they said, and disappeared.

About a week later, I was summoned back to CBS. The writers asked me to read through a short skit with them, to see how it worked. I liked the little scene and thought I could handle it.

I was scheduled to appear the following Tuesday, and instructed to come to the studio at 9 o'clock Monday to rehearse the skit with Alan Copeland, a singer with the Modernaires, the regular group on Uncle Bob's show.

Alan, who remains with the group, joined the Modernaires in 1948, and enjoyed a stellar career both with them and, later, with his own Alan Copeland Singers. He also served for more than 20 years as choral director for Uncle Bing's Christmas specials.

When I went to the rehearsal room to meet with Alan and the other cast members, I was, if not a nervous wreck, certainly an anxious one.

But everyone was as nice and helpful as they could be. We started the run-through, and one of the writers said, "My God! You know your lines!"

Alan was reading from the script, but then Alan was an old pro at this TV stuff and could be ready in a very short time. I, on the other hand, was treating this like I was doing Shakespeare.

Everything went smoothly, to my great relief. And I suddenly realized that I was going to be on "live" TV, my professional debut.

The publicity machine was set in motion. A blurb in *The Oakland Tribune* had it that, "Alameda's Carolyn Miller, the Paramount starlet, gets a big break tomorrow. She'll be on the coast-to-coast Bob Crosby television show. Carolyn's singing and doing a skit with Alan Copeland. The Crosby rating should jump up to there. After all, the Carolyn Miller Fan Club (all former San Jose State pals), is mailing out postcards like mad. "See OUR girl!" they urge proudly. "Remember, you knew her when."

I arrived at CBS at about 10:30 a.m. the following day, and was told to go to the dressing room downstairs.

While Uncle Bob's show was fairly successful, that success didn't extend to a wardrobe or make-up department, so I was responsible for transforming myself into a TV star. Or, at least, into what I thought a TV star looked like.

After I had finished becoming presentable, I sat nervously and waited for someone to call me with a 15-minute warning, something like they do in the theater.

But nothing happened.

Increasingly apprehensive, I jumped on the elevator and rode upstairs to the backstage area.

Suddenly, somebody grabbed me and said, "You're on!"

Oh, God!

It's just a good thing I was a trouper. The skit, which involved my working behind the counter in a record store that sold only Crosby recordings and gave me a chance to trade a few choruses with Alan, went very well and was over in a flash.

I was pleased that I managed to draw some pretty good laughs from the studio audience, especially when I mentioned the then-dismal performance of the Pittsburgh Pirates, in which most everyone knew Uncle Bing had an interest. The set decorator had hung a framed picture of Bing on the wall behind me, and when I mentioned the baseball team, Bing's photo fell to the floor. As a sight gag, it's still pretty funny.

Uncle Bing didn't see the show, but thinking back, that was probably just as well.

My mother, of course, had alerted nearly everyone she knew that her daughter was going to be on TV. When she called me that night with praise and pride, she inquired if I was going to be on the show again.

"I don't know," I said. "It depends on the fan mail."

"What do you mean?"

"The front office said if they got positive fan mail about me, if people write in and say they'd like to see me perform again, and then I'll be invited back."

"Oh, I see," said mother.

She sure did!

A week later, I returned to CBS, to the payroll department, to pick up my check for the appearance. The clerk also handed me some envelopes held together with a rubber band.

"What's this?" I asked her.

"It's your *fan mail!*" she said.

I waited until I got out to my car to examine the letters.

Sure enough, mother had been on the job. Opening up the first five or six of the envelopes, I smiled when I recognized the names of some friends that she had enlisted to write in to Uncle Bob's show, to rave about my performance and request an encore.

The last letter in the group was from a Betty Larson in Santa Monica and was very complimentary. Betty said she liked the idea of Bob having a member of the family on the show, but she didn't like the part in the skit where "poor Bing fell off the wall."

I read it to mother and we both had a good laugh, then mother said, quite seriously, "Honey, who's this Betty Larson?"

"I don't know," I replied. "Isn't she one of your friends?"

"No!" mother said excitedly. "I don't know her! You don't know her! Carolyn, you got a *real fan letter!*"

There surely is nothing like a mother's love.

I was given a darned good review in my hometown paper as well and, yes, I *did* check to make certain mother hadn't written it.

"It would seem practically everybody in the Crosby clan has been touched by the 'divine spark,' that intangible something showpeople believe makes the difference between class and mediocrity," wrote the *Times-Star* critic.

"So we mused while watching Carolyn Miller of Alameda, a niece of Bing and Bob Crosby, as she performed so delightfully on Bob's show yesterday noon with the very talented Alan Copeland of the Modernaires. Under contract to Paramount studios, the attractive Miss Miller has been studying for a movie billing which we are ready to predict she will get in the not-too-distant future. A mimic at an early age, we will always remember Carolyn in her teens doing a takeoff on Billy De Wolfe's 'Mrs. Murgatroyd' and keeping a living room audience in stitches. Carolyn affects the same offhand, easygoing nonchalance so typical of the Crosbys. She has looks, she can sing, and has a flair for comedy as well as drama, all necessary requisites in this exacting era of TV spectaculars and giant movie screens. Make no mistake about it, her talent is such that she can make the big time on her own initiative."

It has been said, that if you start believing your fan mail and reviews, it can ruin you as an actor.

12. BE CAREFUL, IT'S MY HEART

Perhaps my initiative just wasn't *quite* enough.

I learned a great deal while I was at Paramount, about the art of performing, as well as other things. I think I grew up a little bit in that time, and I look back on it as a good, positive, experience, sort of how you reflect on childbirth once you get past the pain.

But that is pretty much all it was. I think I was too sensitive to confront what aspiring actors have to confront in Hollywood. I watched some of the girls at the Studio Club go through all kinds of hell to "make it," strict dieting, daily workouts, nose jobs, and of course insults and rejection after rejection. They had tough hides, a lot of those gals. I don't think my own hide was tough enough to withstand the constant struggle.

One day I came to the difficult realization that, while I might be a pretty proficient "living room entertainer", I lacked the driving desire that makes for success in the movies or on television. It was time to hang up my tap shoes.

So with a little regret and a little relief, I left Paramount when my contract year was up and went hunting for a "real job", leaving behind any thoughts of a career in show business.

As it turned out, I managed to corral myself a little something on the fringes.

One of my girlfriends at the Studio Club was a receptionist at CBS Television City; she had recently become engaged and was planning to leave her job. She asked me if I'd like to have it.

I jumped at the chance. I had, after all, worked at CBS before, all of one day, so I could easily find my way to the corner of Beverly Blvd. and Fairfax Ave.

I settled into "L.A. Working Girl Mode" and found that I really enjoyed running the front desk at such a prestigious address. And I had a talisman of power: the magic button under the desk that released the locked gate, allowing a visitor entry into the inner sanctums of the Columbia Broadcasting System.

At about this time, I took stock of my young life. Not so bad, I thought. I had a good job in an exciting place, a boyfriend just out of the Navy, and plenty of family nearby in case I got myself into a jam.

I was naïve; things would get rougher. But for the moment, seeing the world from the front desk at CBS offered me a pretty nice view and romance was in the air.

My boyfriend and I married about a year after I left Paramount and we rented a small apartment. Uncle Bing had Georgie send us some very nice and welcome wedding gifts. Although our financial future looked fairly bleak, we genuinely felt we could fashion a good life together and we moved forward.

When I learned I was expecting a child, aunt June, uncle Bob's wife, hosted a surprise baby shower, another example of how generous my Crosby relatives were towards me. I turned again to Uncle Bing and asked him if he could suggest a good doctor for me. I was still fairly new to Southern California and had little idea of who might be competent and trustworthy. Besides, Bing seemed to know just about everybody worth knowing.

He instantly and heartily recommended his own physician, Dr. Arnold Stevens. "Dr. Steve's the best," he told me. "He's never let me down."

The problem was, Dr. Stevens's office was in plush Beverly Hills, and my husband and I lived in the Hollywood area. There were several miles between me and medical attention. But I really had little choice at the time, so we enlisted "Dr. Steve" to take care of me and, eventually, to deliver my baby.

That Christmas, Uncle Bing called and invited us to his home for refreshments and Yuletide carols, "I'm having a few friends in" he said. How marvelous I thought, to escape our small apartment for an evening and spend it back at Mapleton Drive. Allan Fisher, Bing's butler, greeted us at the door and gestured towards the living room. There, at the far end stood a choir of at least 25 carolers. Their voices were superb, the music filled the entire house, it was like being in church during high Mass.

I was surprised and touched one day, close to my baby's delivery date, when Uncle Bing called to invite us to stay at his home. "Look at it logically," he said. "You'll be a lot closer to Dr. Steve, and the hospital, and Georgie will be around to help you out."

I was, for the umpteenth time, taken aback by his kindness. Seldom was a man as busy as he was, particularly in those days when he was concurrently wrapped up in movies, radio, television, sports, charity events, personal appearances and, lord knows, keeping track of the four boys. And yet he somehow found time to be responsive to those who needed him, often in quite unexpected ways.

I told him how grateful we were, but, as always, it seemed I was unable to adequately express my thanks. Already feeling blessed, we moved our quarters to Mapleton Drive to await the blessed event.

The day my son was born, Uncle Bing phoned the hospital while I was in the delivery room to check on my progress. There was no way he would have dropped by in person. He hated hospitals, almost as much as he hated funerals.

The nurse who took the call, not one of "Dr. Steve's" regulars, returned to the delivery room and said to the doctor, "Some guy just called—said he was Bing Crosby! He wanted to know if Carolyn had her baby yet."

"Well, it probably *was* Bing Crosby," Dr. Stevens said matter-of-factly. "This patient is Bing's niece."

"Oh, my gosh!" cried the nurse. "I thought it was a joke, so I hung up on him!"

As motherhood was an entirely new role for me, my mother thought I could use an experienced helper. With that advice came her check for $200.00. Through Dr. Steve's office I found Violet, a charming English woman who became our major domo in short order. Her outspoken manner was one of the qualities we liked best about her. One day I asked her if she found our country very different from her own, especially in the area of language and slang expressions. "In the first place," she began, "what you call thread, we call cotton, what you call cookies, we call biscuits and what you call tea, we call dishwater." Violet had us all trained in no time. When I related her remarks to Uncle Bing, he gave a hearty laugh and said, "I've always loved the British!"

My firstborn was hardly the last. By this time my husband and I had moved from Los Angeles to northern California, where job opportunities for him were better and we could live closer to our parents. The next several years were a genuine struggle for us, as we had five more children, born very closely together.

My mother and my mother-in-law helped me with the household and children, in what amounted to our private pre-school, whenever they could. However, they both were getting on in years and my mother lived an hour away.

After a visit to our house one weekend, and watching me attempt to perform the daily chores while trying to maintain some sort of control over my children, my mother had had enough. Unbeknownst to me, she sought Uncle Bing's assistance. "Carolyn could sure use some help," she told him.

"With that many little ones I should say she could. What does she need?"

"Bing," said mother, "just a little extra money for a cleaning woman once a month would go a long way toward lightening her load".

My Benefactor

Uncle Bing agreed, and assured her that he would "call the office."

Soon, a check for $100 arrived in my mailbox, along with a note assuring me that another check for the same amount would arrive each and every month, as Bing's gift for the proper maintenance of my children and household. I was thrilled, and terribly humbled.

About a year and a half later, mother called Uncle Bing again, to ask him to increase the amount of money he was sending me. "You know," she said, "a hundred dollars doesn't go very far these days."

Bing said he certainly understood that.

The following month, when the check arrived, it was for $200.

How could I ever thank him?

I did the best I could. Finally, I sat down and wrote him a letter in which I tried my hardest to express my gratitude for all that he had done for me. I even gave him a careful accounting of exactly how I spent the money.

I imagine he had a good chuckle over my list of figures precisely detailing the spending of two hundred dollars, but I so hoped my letter would give Uncle Bing at least a halfway decent idea of how much he meant to me.

13. FAR AWAY PLACES

We eventually settled in Watsonville, a small town in northern California, south of San Francisco and about an hour's drive from Pebble Beach, which made it possible for me to continue helping mother at Uncle Bing's Pro-Am golf tournament each year.

It was good to be closer to mother's home in Carmel, as well as Uncle Bing's lavish place at Hillsborough, which he had purchased in 1963, shortly before the death of Grandma Kate.

"The Boss" passed away in January, 1964, at the ripe old age of 90. She had been in failing health for several years, and had suffered a series of debilitating strokes. Her last three weeks were spent in a coma.

Grandma Kate's own notoriety was such that her obituary crossed the AP wire and appeared in newspapers coast to coast. It noted that, "Mrs. Crosby was a devout churchgoer and frowned on liquor as a sin. To her death, her married daughters dared not light a cigarette in her presence.

"Yet, as son Larry disclosed with a twinkle in his eye, in late years Kate enjoyed a touch of sherry in her eggnog and she always kept an ounce of bourbon handy, "in case of earthquake," as she put it."

It's somewhat ironic that, following Grandma Kate's death, Uncle Bing would settle down in temblor country, but then he always kept quite a good stock of earthquake medication on hand.

It seems to me that, over the years, mother and I visited all of Uncle Bing's residences, except perhaps the ones he maintained in Mexico. Bing encouraged his family to use any of his properties for a getaway or a vacation, if it was available.

Toward the end of her life, Uncle Bing gave "The Boss" a birthday party. Al of her children were there. From left, standing, are Everett, Bing, Larry, Ted and Bob. Seated with Kate are Kay, left, and Mary Rose.

My first memory of one of Uncle Bing's homes is the estate at Toluca Lake, a small residential area in an old part of Los Angeles, where Bob Hope also lived, and Amelia Earhart had once dwelled. Toluca Lake had its beginnings as a real estate development in the 1920s, its advertising emphasized fly-fishing possibilities and quickly became attractive to those who had enough in their bank account to be able to afford the mortgage. Others who made their homes there at one time or another included W.C. Fields, Frank Sinatra, Doris Day and James Garner.

Uncle Bing purchased a home for his parents in Toluca Lake, as well, so it was a natural destination for the entire clan. His own 20-room (and seven-bathroom!) mansion at 10500 Camarillo Street became one of the more talked-about area homes, the subject of a much-distributed postcard which, I found to my amusement, folks are still hawking on E-bay. It was also an important dot on those maps to the movie stars' homes, which seemed at one point to be available on every street corner in Southern California.

I visited the Toluca Lake house on a few occasions when I was nine or ten years old, spending much of my time swimming in its pool with my cousins and the neighborhood gang.

Uncle Bing also would occasionally take us to the nearby Lakeside Country Club, which had been a premier attraction for Los Angeles area duffers since 1924 and where he and Hope spent quite a lot of time lining up their putts.

Dennis, Phil, Gary Crosby, Grandma Kate's brother, Jack Crosby, Carolyn and Marilyn.

At Lakeside, mother and Grandma Kate would sit conversing at the glass-topped patio table, keeping an eye on me while I went swimming.

Then, around noon or so, they would order lunch, which was delivered to them by a waiter in a starched white serving jacket, a detail which still speaks to me of upper-class elegance.

Postcard for Uncle Bing's Toluca Lake home

Examining golf trophies at Lakeside

Later in the afternoon I was allowed to order a chocolate soda, and this wonderful waiter brought it to me on his sparkling silver tray while I sat at the edge of the pool. I felt very fortunate indeed.

Newspaper coverage of Bing's house fire

Uncle Bing's Toluca Lake home was destroyed in a fire, caused, ironically, by a short circuit in some Christmas tree lights, on January 2, 1943. Dixie and the boys, along with Georgie and a house guest were all in the home when the fire started. It was about three or four in the afternoon. Everyone got out safely before the roof fell in. The tragedy was big news and the photos filled a full page in the Los Angeles Times. One side note is that uncle Bing had stashed some cash in one of his shoes, after a winning day at the races. He viewed the fire damage, then went upstairs to retrieve the money. No doubt he was darn glad the funds were spared, close to two thousand dollars, to see another day at the track.

Uncle Bing entertains Cass Daley and a group of reporters at the Elko, Nevada, and world premiere of Here Comes the Groom.

14. DON'T FENCE ME IN

When I was 12 or 13 years old, we made a visit to one of Uncle Bing's ranches near Elko, Nevada, and, let me tell you, *this* was hardly Lakeside!

It was, according to Uncle Bing, "one of the last bastions of the Old West."

History records that Uncle Bing had been at the ranching life since 1942, when he sealed a deal to buy what was then the Jube Wright Ranch. This became the first of what would eventually become seven Elko County ranches which ran the "Cross-B" brand.

Bing at his Elko ranch

Dixie helps Bing with Key to the City of Elko, Nevada

In years to come, he would put Elko County on the map, serving as the City of Elko's honorary mayor, and even holding the world premiere of one of his movies, 1951's *Here Comes the Groom*, in Elko.

Movie poster for premier in Elko

On that occasion, described as the biggest movie premiere since *Gone with the Wind*'s famous send-off in Atlanta, Paramount flew in the governors of Utah and Nevada and hundreds of reporters from newspapers across the country. The festivities culminated in a live national broadcast on CBS Radio, called *The Elko Show*.

That was an enormous deal for a town which only numbered about five thousand souls.

There is no doubt at all that Elko County and my uncle enjoyed a strong, mutual love affair, which lasted a decade and a half. Uncle Bing called northeastern Nevada "my favorite corner of the globe."

Bing bringing home the mail at the ranch

Bing and his four ranch hands

Who's this cowboy?

Bing at his Elko ranch

In Elko, he had the anonymity he craved, discovering to his delight that, once folks got used to seeing him around town, they treated him as just another citizen of their high desert community. He made good friends, among them hotelier Newton Crumley and real estate man John Oldham, and he would often take them along on his outdoor adventures.

Bing sorting mail at the ranch

One of Bing's favorite gag writers, Barney Dean, once related a story which characterized Bing's relationship with his adopted town. Apparently, my uncle had imbibed a bit of Christmas cheer one evening close to the holiday, and dropped by a local store to serenade the shoppers with an impromptu chorus of "White Christmas."

Gratified by his warm reception, "he got everybody in town out of bed to sing Christmas carols," Dean said.

My own encounter with Elko came after Bing acquired the sprawling PX Ranch, a spread he was obviously proud of, proud enough to ring up mother one day and invite us out to see it.

Bing fixing fence on his Elko ranch

"Come up this summer," Bing said. "You'll get a chance to see what goes on there. Maybe the boys will be branding, or doing a round-up or something."

"Oh great!" I thought. "a home on the range!"

Bing and Lindsay ride on the Elko ranch

We did go that summer and it was a very, very long drive for me as a young teenager perched expectantly in the back seat, in full "are we there yet?" mode.

This was cattle country, the real thing, not some posh dude ranch, but with miles upon miles of sagebrush and hardscrabble desert ground.

Bing and Lindsay at the Elko ranch

Elko lay about halfway between Reno and Salt Lake City. The town was small, but it seemed to have just about everything anyone would need.

The only thing was, Uncle Bing's PX Ranch was way out yonder. The turn you made off the main road to get to the operation was indicated only by a mile marker, and so you really had to watch for it.

The ranch house was quite modest, no spiral staircases or swimming pools here. But Uncle Bing could whack golf balls for as long and as far as he wanted out there in the sagebrush and never even hit one of his cattle.

Bing riding steer

Bing rides out in front of the Elko ranch house

There were several buildings on the property, small houses to accommodate the ranch hands, sheds for tools and equipment, stables and barns for the horses and other livestock.

Oh, and one additional facility that wasn't common to most Elko County ranches, a recording studio.

But the best place of all was the cookhouse. I can't remember how many cowboys I counted at lunch there one day, maybe a dozen or so—and when the bowls and platters of food came out of the kitchen, my eyes popped.

Pork chops piled high, mounds of potatoes, huge bowls of beans, fresh corn by the platefuls, a plentitude of pancakes, and the tallest mountain of scrambled eggs I had ever seen at one time in my life.

It went on and on.

Gallons of coffee, of course and, I recall, about four kinds of pie—two tins of each. These boys were sure were hungry.

As a typical kid, I was a little disappointed that there was no place to swim and no chance to visit a soda shop. But I contented myself during our stay with what was at hand and found surprising fun in activities like riding horses and climbing up high in the hay barn and jumping into the cushioning piles of straw below.

Gary, Phil, Lindsay and Bing with friends

Uncle Bing loved his ranches, and the ranching life. He wasn't at all afraid of doing the hard work himself, either. He had hoped that one or all of his boys might take up the life, but none of them seemed interested and he sold the ranches in the late 1950s. Even so, Elko residents still recall that he kept in touch with them over the later years, often surprising them with unexpected phone calls, letters, and Christmas cards.

Uncle Bing's house at Hayden Lake, Idaho, was another delightfully remote getaway. We traveled there twice when I was in my mid-teens, and to say Hayden

Lake boasted "scenic beauty" was shortchanging it. Located east of Bing's old stomping grounds, Spokane, and just over the Idaho border, the property was covered with pines and other evergreens, giving it a summer camp sort of feeling.

Hayden Lake was a popular place for the young crowd and their families. There was an outdoor amphitheater that showed movies almost every night. I loved it there. I think I had my first summer romance at Hayden Lake.

Inviting us out for our first visit, Uncle Bing informed mother she could stay as long as she wanted because he'd be tied up filming a picture, *A Connecticut Yankee in King Arthur's Court*, I believe and would be staying on in Los Angeles that summer.

The house had two or three levels and was built on a slope, slipped in among trees, and right on the lake. You hiked a long set of wooden stairs to get down to the boat dock.

The most handsome Chris Craft motorboat was stored in the boat house, bobbing gently up and down in the water. From the second I saw it, I knew it was just begging me to take it out for a spin. But first, I had to be taught to handle it, of course, and I had to get permission every time I used it, which meant I had to ask Mrs. Lemon, the Georgie of Hayden Lake, as she came with the place.

Another busy, no-nonsense gal, the Scottish Mrs. Lemon cooked and cleaned for us during our stay, and made the best scones this side of Glascow. She saw no problem with me becoming skipper of the Crosby Chris Craft, just as long as I was careful with it.

I was out on the lake every day in that sleek boat, sometimes by myself and sometimes with a friend or family member who came to join us during our stay. Often, we went water skiing, other times I would dive off the boat and just enjoy swimming for awhile in the sun-dappled water. Thanks to Uncle Bing, I had a very good summer and a great tan.

Years later, my cousin Phil, one of Bing's twins, bought the house and stayed there many times. He used it as a second home.

Uncle Bing

15. ADESTE FIDELIS

Uncle Bing's final residence was his sumptuous living quarters on Jackling Road, in Hillsborough, in the San Francisco Bay area. It was a lovely, French-style mansion that he and his second family called home.

A few years after he and Kathryn and the kids, Harry, Nathaniel and Mary Frances, had settled in, around 1971 or 1972, Bing phoned mother and said, "Now that we live closer, why don't we all get together at Christmastime? I'll call Kay, and both of you bring your families—how about 12 o'clock on the 23rd?"

Uncle Bing himself snapped this photo of his son Nathaniel, far right, and his Crosby cousins at play on the Hillsborough gridiron.

With that first invitation, the annual holiday gathering became a much-anticipated and treasured experience for us.

I know it was for Uncle Bing. I could tell right away when we arrived and found him at the door to greet us, all smiles. My boys were dressed in shirts, ties and jackets, but they had brought along sports bags containing a couple of footballs and casual clothes. When all five came barreling through the door, Uncle Bing shouted brightly, "I see the team has arrived!"

After they had all changed clothes, Harry and Nathaniel joined my boys for a game on the back lawn, and Bing grabbed his camera, happily exclaiming, "I gotta get a picture of this!"

Uncle Bing's characteristic informality seemed to clash with his new surroundings. This Hillsborough house was some place! It felt much more staid and proper to me than his other residences. In exterior appearance it was much like an elaborate chateau, and European touches were in evidence throughout its winding halls. It was once the home of Charles Howard, owner of the legendary racehorse Seabiscuit.

Bing and Kathryn's home in Hillsborough

A right turn at the grand entrance led you to the study, where we adults would typically gather to chit-chat while the kids expended their energy outside. These were lively conversations, with Uncle Bing injecting his usual good humor and pointed questions. As always, he was genuinely interested in what was going on with us. I have to laugh somewhat ruefully when I read accounts of how "distant" Bing was, how "disengaged." That is so far from the actual man that we knew, it seems almost as if an entirely different person is being described.

If anything, he was *too* engaged. While he may have appeared distant to some, that might have been because he was at that moment worrying about one of his children, or grandchildren, or nieces, for that matter. Perhaps he was mulling through a musical arrangement he wasn't happy with, or fretting about a horse that had come up lame, or considering the effect of new grazing regulations on one of his ranches. He might have been daydreaming about new advances in recording, running his lines for a movie, or sweating through a difficult trade involving his beloved Pittsburgh Pirates.

Perhaps, later in life, he was troubled about hitting the notes he had hit effortlessly twenty years before, I'm quite certain he was, in fact. Maybe he kept rerunning that putt he had missed today, or kicking himself because he had forgotten someone's birthday or some other personal occasion. He may have been concerned about a friend's alcohol problem, fisheries pollution, or the logistics of a concert tour. He might have been sweating a nagging detail involving his golf tournament, or puzzling over a business reversal.

I sometimes wonder, too, if my uncle wasn't afraid of being hurt, both personally and professionally, and so had built up some pretty fancy defense mechanisms over the years to hold back heartbreak.

I have a letter Uncle Bing wrote to mother after her husband, J.T., suffered a heart attack. It is like many such letters Uncle Bing wrote to his family and friends, reassuring them and offering his help:

> *Dear Mary Rose:*
>
> *I'm dictating this from Las Cruces where I just got your letter with the sad news about Jim and his very serious coronary attack.*
>
> *This must be a really shattering experience for you, and Kathryn and I really are terribly concerned.*
>
> *I hope Jim doesn't rush it now, and try to get up and about too soon, but will listen to the doctor's advice.*
>
> *Don't worry about the future, because you can depend on me to take care of this as far as you're concerned.*
>
> *All our love now, and don't let this shocking event get you down.*
>
> *Love, Bing*

Distant, some called him? Consider the distance my uncle had to go, every single day. That he met his responsibilities as well as he did is a tribute to his intellect, his drive, and his spirit.

And to think Bing Crosby was globally famous for being "laid-back."

During those family talks at Hillsborough, Uncle Bing seldom bothered to discuss his own problems or troubles. Usually, when he wasn't quizzing one of us about our own lives, he was offering a hilarious tale about grouse hunting with Phil Harris, or detailing his plans to go on safari, or deep sea fishing off the coast of Baja, once he finished whatever project was occupying his time at the moment.

Christmas dinner—Bing grabs his camera

His study was full of souvenirs from those adventurous occasions he enjoyed when he broke away from the pressures of being Bing. He had a myriad of friends in all walks of life that he could call on to join him in any of the pursuits he enjoyed. He had golfing buddies, hunting and fishing buddies, and baseball buddies, many of whom were pictured on the walls around us, posing with him and their various trophies. The den also boasted a collection of Western paintings, in the style of Remington and Russell, and cabinets filled with golf memorabilia.

The host and hostess at Christmastime in Hillsborough

Our Christmas parties followed a joyous routine. Shortly after our arrival, butler Alan Fisher would bring in a large punch bowl of "holiday cheer." After we were sufficiently cheered, Uncle Bing would announce that we should all retire to the living room to sing Christmas carols. He always hired a pianist to accompany us in our festive sing-along.

People don't sing together much these days. More is the pity. I recall that the kids in the group always were just a little bit hesitant at first, not sure if they should join in. But, at the strenuous urging of Uncle Bing, myself, and the other adults on hand, they eventually got with the program.

As you might imagine, the musical session was always closed by Uncle Bing. He would stand next to the piano and sing "White Christmas" with a simple piano accompaniment, sans toupee and any pretense. I can see him still, hear him still, and it is a memory I return to every holiday season.

When dinner was announced, we'd all troop down the hall to the dining room. I counted 23 of us that first year, the first time the family had gathered together in ages. Uncle Bing seemed as thrilled as we all were to have the clan under his roof.

Bing and Kathryn perform at one of our family Christmas parties

He continued hosting the Christmas party for five or six years. Sometimes my Uncle Larry and other family members we hadn't seen in recent days would join us, or Bing's in-laws, the Grandstaffs.

One year, Uncle Bing surprised us. As we engaged in our usual catching-up before dinner, he announced that he would like to hear something from every one who was there, a song, a joke or a story.

His son, Harry, was taking guitar lessons at the time, and Bing asked him to perform a certain song that he enjoyed. "I'll have to go get my other guitar," Harry said.

"That kid has more guitars than Segovia," Bing said, and the place broke up.

When Uncle Bing called on me, I went absolutely blank. I couldn't think of a thing to do, or say, or sing. Here I was, the family's accomplished "living room entertainer," completely at a loss. Uncle Bing raised his infamous left eyebrow and offered me one of his cheery little frowns, no one ever frowned as happily as he did, just witness any "Road" picture, and moved on to the next contestant.

Just wait 'til next year, I vowed.

At the next holiday party, the procedure was pretty much the same, only this time, perhaps remembering the preceding Christmas and thinking he was doing me a favor, Uncle Bing skipped over me! I was crushed.

Because this time I was indeed prepared, in fact, my family and I had rehearsed our holiday number for *two solid weeks!*

The next thing I knew, dinner was being served. When we had finished the first course, I decided I would simply have to be bold about this. I tapped my wine glass with a spoon and said, "Uncle Bing, you didn't ask me to do anything this year, and I wanted you to know that, this time, I'm ready!"

Uncle Bing chuckled. "Well, fine," he said. "Let's hear it now."

My family and I surprised Uncle Bing—who took this photo— with a spirited rendition of "Oh, Tannenbaum" in German, no less

The children and I stood together behind our chairs and on my downbeat, burst into "Oh Tannenbaum", entirely in German.

Anyone who has ever had to deal with teaching children a Christmas carol in English surely must realize the extent of our preparation for this festive moment!

Mother was sitting next to Bing, and they both broke out in hearty laughter and applause. Uncle Bing excused himself saying, as usual, "I've got to get my camera!"

This kind of get-together, where everybody chimed in offering some sort of entertainment, was standard operating procedure for the Crosby family. It had its genesis in the Sunday gatherings with music and song which were a big part of Bing's upbringing, an Irish tradition he carried on.

Uncle Larry very beautifully described those shindigs in an essay he wrote upon Grandpa Harry's death in 1950. The family, too long apart, had reunited for the funeral, and gathered together afterwards to recapture the spirit of their youthful days together.

I have the essay still, and reprint it below. I think no one has ever done a better job than Uncle Larry of describing the camaraderie that music inspired in the Crosby family:

ONE SUNDAY EVENING

In the early years of the Crosby family, nearly every Sunday evening found the family circle complete in an atmosphere of play, and banter, and music. After the supper dishes had been cleared away, perhaps one of the youngsters would start up the phonograph... that early model with the long horn, an extravagance that Dad blithely claimed someone had given him, fully-aware that none of us believed him. Or Dad would play his mandolin or guitar, warming up with a nonsensical ditty we knew only as "Sing-Song Polly Catch a Ky-mee-oh." And soon everyone would be singing.

And now, after the family had been scattered for many years, they were all together again, closing ranks, as they assembled at Everett's home for Sunday dinner. Here were Mother, Larry and Elaine and their children, Molly and Jack and Jack's wife Bea; Everett and Florence; Ted; Bing and Dixie and their four sons, Gary, Phillip, Dennis and Lindsay; Catherine and Eddie Mullin; Mary Rose, Bob and June and their Cathy; Florence's father, George Guthrie, and Father Sugrue.

As usual, there was much banter and kidding during the dinner and as usual, Everett and Mary Rose were generally on the receiving end, and they held their own, as of old. Someone suggested a song and the show was on, with Mother beating time much in the fashion she uses her racing program to bring in her horse.

First Bing and Gary sang a duet... someone brought out a ukulele... and a Crosby Sunday evening was in full swing as various members of the family and their children took turns at song. Phillip and Dennis sang a duet and Linny, after some coaxing, gave out with a solo with Bing backing him up. Cathy sang "Dear Hearts and Gentle People" and Bob joined in. Larry did a parody on "You Wore A Tulip," and Mary Rose, after being teased with a chorus of "Anchor's Aweigh" (in honor of her seafaring husband), joined Bing in a number. Dixie dug up "Has Anybody Seen My Gal," Jack and Bea jitterbugged.

Then, after dessert, when everyone moved into the playroom, Florence sat at the piano and delighted with several songs. The gathering broke up as Bing took Gary, Phillip and Dennis, and Ted and Eddie Mullin, to catch a northbound train.

It was the kind of a Sunday evening Dad liked best . . . good food, music, and laughter with his family gathered around him, for he would have echoed the sentiments of the poet who wrote:

> *"No funeral gloom, my dears, when I am gone*
> *Corpse-gazings, tears, black raiment, graveyard grimness;*
> *Think of me as withdrawn into the dimness,*
> *Yours still, you mine; remember all the best*
> *Of our past moments; and forget the rest;*
> *And so, to where I wait, come gently on."*

Yes, there were banter and songs, but underneath and each to himself, some serious thoughts and good resolutions. To help us keep these, we have an advance man loaded with spiritual bouquets, thousands of masses, more than he needs. He will spare a few, even if he must get along with a bum string or two on his harp. (End of essay).

Uncle Bing's Hillsborough Christmas parties always ended where they had begun, in the entry hall, where gifts would be exchanged. Sometimes there was a table set up with items to choose from for the children, who of course loved that portion of the festivities. And then there were the wrapped gifts for the adults, never anything ostentatious, just nice, thoughtful things.

Too soon, it was time to leave, time for a few tears and a lot of laughter and kisses and handshakes as we expressed our thanks to Uncle Bing and Kathryn for a lovely party. I can still hear our voices echoing there in the hall, sharing the comfy rapport that only families are privy to, and then we would be off to our separate homes, still so excited by our holiday reunion that we would phone each other to rehash the events of the evening. "Wasn't the dessert wonderful?" "I still can't believe you told THAT joke!" "Don't you think Uncle Bing looks great?"

For all the world, Uncle Bing was synonymous with Christmas, and those times of sharing it with him were like priceless gifts. All of us who were there reopen those packages each December, and we pull from them memories merry and bright.

16. REMEMBER ME

As the 1970s wore on, Uncle Bing seemed fairly content with his life as the Squire of Hillsborough. He still kept busy with his golf tournament, his television specials, and his many sporting and business interests, but he did little recording, and very rarely performed in public. We noticed that he had slowed down.

Raising a new set of youngsters and hoping this time to do all the right things as a parent, played a key role in his retreat. The 1966 death of his brother Everett, the man whose headlong determination had guided Uncle Bing throughout his career, also played a factor.

I call it a retreat, but it wasn't a full-scale one by any means. Uncle Bing hardly lacked for exposure. It was during those years that he, Kathryn and the children became American icons in a completely unexpected way, appearing in popular commercials for, what else?—Minute Maid Orange Juice. These 60-second vignettes of domestic bliss complete with 100 percent of your Vitamin-C requirement attracted a new generation of fans to Bing's easygoing style and charming repartee.

What was missing was the music.

It would return, for a short, but very sweet time.

In 1974, Uncle Bing fought a nearly-fatal battle with nocardia, a virulent fungus that had invaded his lungs. His doctors discovered and removed a tumor the size of an orange and a good bit of his left lung, in eradicating the disease.

That was bad enough; it didn't help when, once that danger was past, he broke a rib in a fall while recuperating at the hospital.

8x10 glossy photo sent to fans

Upon his recovery, perhaps seeing his near-brush with death as a wake-up call to get back into life, Uncle Bing returned to the world of entertainment in a very big way.

Seeking to recapture his glory days for that new generation attuned to him, he worked quickly, lining up concerts in New York, Los Angeles, and other major U.S. cities, and a triumphant return to England and Ireland, which had always greeted him with open arms. He took to the studio as well, recording a number of well-received albums, including one with his old friend Fred Astaire.

In a 1976 appearance on the *Tonight Show*, remarkably the lone occasion he perched on Johnny Carson's couch, Uncle Bing said, "The reason I started to do some personals, was that I was coming out of NBC about three or four months ago, and some guy came up to me, some fan, and he said, 'Didn't you used to be Bing Crosby?' I said, 'I've gotta get back in action, I've gotta do something to remedy this.'"

Later that year, Uncle Bing phoned mother and said his butler, Alan Fisher, would help make arrangements if she wanted to attend the opening night of his performance at the London Palladium. Bing said he would appreciate her being there, to share his re-acquaintance with his British audience. "It should be a sold-out performance," he told her. "Let me know if you can make it."

Mother told Bing she didn't need to be asked twice, it would be the thrill of her life.

"I'm so glad you're going!" I told her when I heard the news.

"But I want you to go with me," mother said. "I'll pay the expenses if you plan the trip."

What could I say to an offer like that?

I floated around in a fog of sheer disbelief. A couple of days later I managed to cut through the haze enough to drive over to Carmel. Mother and I sat down with her travel agent to make some arrangements.

She was simply so excited there was no containing her. "I'm going over to London to hear my brother Bing sing!" she enthused to the amused agent.

We decided that we should extend our trip in order to visit cities and countries we had always dreamed about. We would tour England, then Ireland, the birthplace of some of our ancestors, and then investigate France and parts of Italy.

Mother had been suffering from a vision problem in recent years. Her eyesight was failing her, so I was especially thankful to Uncle Bing for suggesting she make the trip now, while she would still be able to see the beauty of Europe and the United Kingdom, and while she could still watch him perform. Mother made certain that one of the stops on our journey would be a visit to the grotto at Lourdes, so she could bathe her eyes in the miraculous waters there. Her Catholic faith was still alive and well.

As for me, I was so wound-up in anticipation of our overseas adventure that I hardly slept on the plane to London.

Upon our arrival, we were greeted by a most charming Irish gentleman by the name of George O'Reilly, who at Bing's request drove us from the airport to our hotel, where we enjoyed dinner with George and his wife.

George was Bing's producer, friend, travel planner, aide de camp, theatrical agent and promoter in Ireland and the U.K., and he did a marvelous job in each category. He was a charmer as well. Another native of the British Isles, Alan Fisher, was dispatched the next day to take us sightseeing. Being born to the territory and all, Alan knew all the best places to show us, as well as all the right shortcuts so we would avoid the heavy London traffic.

It was hardly a wonder that Alan would know his way around. He had, prior to joining Bing and Kathryn's household in the early 1960s, served the Duke and Duchess of Windsor, and Princess Elizabeth before her ascension to the throne.

Following his service to my uncle, Alan would return to England to work for Prince Charles and Princess Diana.

Alan took us to the Mall that leads to Buckingham Palace. To our surprise, the streets were lined with thousands of people and I asked Alan, "Is it always like this? Like every day?"

Alan smiled. "Well," he said, "today is special. I wanted to make certain I got you here in time to see the Queen."

"Oh, my God!" I thought. One day in the country and I'm about to encounter Queen Elizabeth!

It was as if I was having an out-of-body experience or something.

I must have drifted off in my royal reverie, because Alan nudged me, and brought me back to this unreal reality.

"Now, watch her majesty," he said. "She'll wave to her Mum, who is standing in the window of her residence, Clarence House over there."

Sure enough, as the ornate carriage approached from the left and came close to us, the Queen turned her head to the right and waved that familiar white-gloved-one-hand-rocking-back-and-forth gesture which has become so familiar to everyone over the years of her reign.

We spent the rest of the day eyeing one fabulous site after another, as Alan escorted us to the high spots in the heart of the city and then, back at our hotel, we impatiently had a drink and a light supper in preparation for Uncle Bing's Palladium concert.

Mother and I had brought our best dresses for this very special occasion, and I recall that we sounded just like a couple of giddy teenagers as we dressed for the performance, putting on our makeup and jewelry. It was June, the weather was warm, and so we had no need for wraps.

We hardly knew what to expect. We wondered what the theater would be like. Would the audience be polite and restrained, as we had always heard the British people were, or would Uncle Bing receive thunderous applause?

We waited in the hotel lobby and, at the appointed hour, a Rolls Royce pulled up, and the driver opened the door for us.

I reflected during the ride to the theater that this was much like my memorable trip to the Academy Awards 20 years before, both excursions made possible by my Uncle Bing.

We arrived at the Palladium a trifle early, but there was already a small crowd outside. Our seats were about eight rows back from the stage, which proved a perfect location to see everything.

As the audience filed in, I quickly noticed there were people here from all walks of life, working-class to socialites, a pure cross-section of humanity. It was such a testament to Bing's broad appeal that everyone felt as if they were about to see an old friend, who had been away too long.

I learned later that Uncle Bing had ordered ticket prices for the event be kept low and affordable to everyone as a gesture of appreciation to his British fans.

The audience chatted, some in the crowd even read their evening newspapers, while they waited for the curtain to go up. When it did, and the audience caught sight of my uncle, the welcoming applause went on for a couple of minutes, an ovation which his beaming smile showed was very gratifying to him.

When he stood by the piano and sang a medley of some of his most popular songs, my thoughts flew back to our family Christmas dinners at Hillsborough, where he would stand just like that and sing for us. It was the same ingratiating manner that captured both our family and this adoring crowd. Here was Uncle Bing, singing songs they knew by heart, in that voice which defined the century. It was truly beautiful. I was awestruck being there.

At the London Palladium

At intermission, mother and I went to the lobby for refreshments, and I overheard some of the remarks by the people in attendance. One man said to his wife, "The old boy's doing pretty well for his age," as if he was discussing a bloke he had known all his life.

And, in a way, he was.

Billed as "Bing Crosby and Friends," the concert also featured Rosemary Clooney, along with Kathryn, Harry, Nathaniel, and Mary Frances. British Comedian Ted Rogers offered support, along with the Joe Bushkin Quartet and the Pete Moore Orchestra, which had become a real favorite of Uncle Bing's, in both his latter-day recordings and live appearances.

We enjoyed the show immensely and marveled at uncle Bing's stamina, after all, this veteran of stage and screen was in his seventies and the show was about three hours long. Mother and I knew all the songs that were performed that night, even the ones from days of yore when she would have the radio on in the kitchen. As we sat there listening to one tune after another, I caught sight of mother tapping her foot in time to the music.

Later, when we ventured backstage following the lengthy standing ovation which brought the curtain down on the show, Uncle Bing was all smiles and quips, and no one in the crowd of well-wishers were as proud as mother and I to see him return to performing in such spectacular fashion.

Witnessing Uncle Bing give one of the performances of his life was hardly enough for mother, however. She wanted to be out and about every day we had in England. She wanted to see *everything*.

I told her that I'd heard Mel Torme was also in London, appearing at Talk of the Town, and that if she wanted to see him, we ought to make plans.

She did want to go and rang up Uncle Bing to inquire of him precisely how you arranged to see Mel Torme. Uncle Bing must have chuckled a good, long time at that query, but he assured her that Alan Fisher would, as usual, take care of the details. "You just go ahead and have a good time," he said.

When Alan checked in later in the day, he said he had reserved a table for us and advised we should be at the club by 8 o'clock. We had dinner at the hotel and took a taxi.

At Talk of the Town, the maitre d' welcomed us and showed us to a dynamite ringside table. The next thing I knew, a waiter had arrived with a bottle of champagne and a note.

"For Bing's sister," it read. "Compliments of Mel Torme and he welcomes you backstage after the show."

Following his fine performance, we found our way to Torme's dressing room to meet him and thank him for the wine and the music. He was the dearest man, very gentle and kind.

He took mother's hand in his and told her of his great admiration for her brother. It was a simple, genuine moment, and one of the highlights of our trip.

We would make our journey to Ireland, and France, and Italy, but too soon this dream-of-a-lifetime was over, and I returned again to my everyday life, like Judy returning from the Land of Oz.

17. BROTHER, CAN YOU SPARE A DIME?

Watsonville, the small, agricultural town we had settled into in northern California, was an idyllic place to raise a family. My boys had trees to climb in an apple orchard about three blocks away, they could hike down to a creek and collect pollywogs and splash around. A veterinarian operated a clinic right across the street from us, and my children loved seeing people bring their animals to "Doc" for repair and maintenance.

"Doc" was also considered the best horse leg doctor in three counties, and we often watched him treating the ponies, along with cows and goats, in a vacant lot outside his clinic.

We had a black Labrador retriever, cages of English tumbler pigeons and jars of ladybugs and butterflies. It seemed like every day was show and tell around our place. My sons also found the time to be altar boys at church, to pedal their bicycles on paper routes, and to participate in just about every sport imaginable.

Our Tom Sawyer style of life continued for nearly 20 years, until my husband passed away.

Although the children were pretty well grown by this time and I had been teaching school part-time, things were tight and I had been left with very little insurance money.

I had a friend in Albuquerque, New Mexico, who invited me to come out for a visit, to get away from the sad memories and to do some grieving, some thinking and planning for the future.

I drove out of town and pointed myself in the direction of the Great Southwest, wondering if I was crazy to be going on this trip. "It's just a waste of time and money," I thought, and very nearly turned back.

But I had the radio on to the oldies station and wouldn't you know it, they were playing that finger-popping song of Bobby Troup's "Route 66." While it wasn't a Bing Crosby record, it did fill me with the sort of happy reassurance that my uncle's recordings did, and it kept me going East toward Flagstaff, Arizona.

I had never been to this part of the country before, and I found an unexpected beauty in the changes from green rolling hills to scrub oak to high desert dotted with scattered pines. To this day, the red earth mesas just outside of Gallup have a special meaning for me, because they signal the beginning of Indian Country.

It was a country I would become so much a part of, and which in turn would become a part of me.

I had a wonderful visit with my friend, all the while trying to soak up the cultures, smells and flavors of this magnificent place. My friend gave me a crash course in the ways and customs of the indigenous Indians, entertaining me with tales about the pueblo people, as well as the Navajo who lived in the area.

I was fascinated. I wanted to stay longer but my family was waiting for me back home, where mother had been watching the children.

I couldn't get Albuquerque out of my mind, though, and when my friend phoned to offer me a job in her curio shop, I sat the children down at the kitchen table and we talked about relocating to New Mexico.

They didn't want to leave Watsonville, of course, it was the place where they'd grown up, gone to school, made friends. The friends were the difficult part of saying goodbye.

We had been in that house for 17 years, and leaving everything behind to go forward to the unknown was one of the most difficult decisions I've ever had to make.

When the children finally said, "Whatever you think is best, Mom," we left Watsonville.

I would say that we were on a tight budget, but that would indicate that there were any funds to budget at all. I didn't want to ask Uncle Bing for money again— I hoped to do this one on my own.

It's not as if he wouldn't have helped me out. Like all of my family, he was sympathetic to my plight and as I have said, he was quite generous when any of us needed him. Yet, he showed a casual air about his wealth at times. In one case, while having a conversation with his accountant, he asked the man, "what am I worth, anyway?" The accountant looked over the top of his glasses at Bing, a bit startled and replied, "you know Bing, I really don't know either. I'll have to look it up, shall I get back to you.?"

When a member of the clan asked Bing for a loan, he would scrutinize the situation carefully, and if he decided the cause was worthy enough, his accountant would prepare a brief contract which typically would provide the loan at a very low interest rate, it was very much a business transaction.

Unlike the bank, however, Uncle Bing would, when Christmas came around, provide a little holiday bonus to those indebted to him. He would send a letter announcing, "This Christmas, I am forgiving $100 (or $1,000) of your loan. Happy Holidays! Love, Bing."

I recall a time that one of my relatives contacted Uncle Bing, asking for a loan to help her pay for sessions with a psychiatrist. When he asked her what the problem was, she explained that she just couldn't seem to hold down a job.

She would find work, she said, but was constantly late and therefore ended up being fired, time after time.

She said she had found a therapist who assured her that she could be cured of her problem after a number of counseling sessions with him.

Bing thought for a moment. "Well," he finally replied, "sounds like you need a better alarm clock" and turned down her loan request.

If you were in a genuine jam, however, Uncle Bing would usually come through, as occurred when mother got a little too enthusiastic about horse racing. Uncle Bing was a well-known aficionado of the sport, he owned racehorses most of his life and was one of the founders of the famed Del Mar race track and his passion rubbed off on both Grandma Kate and my mother.

Bing and one of his nags

When we visited him in Los Angeles, we frequently attended the races together, lunching in the turf club and cheering our chosen ponies on to victory. I enjoyed the races in L.A. since there was always the added bonus of catching sight of a movie star or two. I still remember how thrilled I was to spot John Wayne on one of our outings.

The problem was, mother liked betting the horses so much that she took it up as a sort of secondary career. Not being Bing Crosby, she really couldn't afford the pastime.

She often took me along as she made the rounds to tracks like Bay Meadows, Tanforan and Santa Anita.

By the time I was a teenager; mother had grown more involved in the Sport of Kings, and had reached a point where she was so far behind financially that she really should have quit.

But she found herself a bookie, instead.

He drove a truck for the local dry cleaners and would stop by our house so frequently to pick up mother's bets that the neighbors must have thought we were serious clean freaks.

I suppose mother was hoping for a winning streak to augment her meager income. She had been selling a line of beauty products at office parties and by appointment in private homes, but it was hardly enough to support us.

Eventually, even mother realized that she was in deep trouble with her betting, and she appealed to Uncle Bing for help.

He asked his usual questions first and then offered her some advice: hunker down and find a career which would provide the income she needed without resorting to wagering on horseflesh.

That having been said, about a week later, he sent Uncle Everett up the coast from L.A., checkbook in hand.

When Everett arrived at our door, I knew instantly that something was wrong. Uncle Ev had never come to visit us before.

He and mother sat at her desk in the dining room, and I was politely instructed to disappear.

Before I did, I saw mother give the bills to Uncle Ev, and he wrote out a check for each one.

It was about that time that my mother heeded Uncle Bing's advice and began studying for an actual trade, as a real estate broker. Her study paid off, and she built a profitable career in the area.

Shortly after Uncle Ev's errand of mercy, mother received a large manila envelope. She opened it and pulled out a publicity photo of Uncle Bing.

It wasn't the usual happy-go-lucky promo shot. In this one, Bing eyed the camera with looks that could kill.

He had inscribed the photo "To Mary Rose: Here's the way I look when I hear you've been to the track, Love, Bing."

That nasty look

18. THE SINGING HILLS

Determined to do it my way, I arrived in Albuquerque with six children, six hundred dollars, and a job.

I rented a small house, enrolled the children in school for the fall semester, and I went to work. And did I ever *work!* I was so busy with my job and taking care of the house and the kids, I had very little time for socializing.

I was fortunate that there was a nice couple, George and Linda, who had a shop next door to where I was working, and they reached out to me in friendship.

George and Linda owned a very attractive store, and their success had allowed them to open two other locations. One of them was in the original section of Albuquerque known as Old Town, where charming adobe homes and haciendas had been converted by their new owners into quaint shops and boutiques.

One day, George came to me and said he was going to relocate one of his shops in Old Town, and asked if I liked that area.

I told him I didn't like it. I loved it.

"Well," George said, "would you like to take over my old location there?"

"Of course I would," I said. But there was nagging reality to be considered. "I know you'll be asking a fair amount for that spot, there's hardly ever a vacancy," I told him. "I'd have to buy my way in, right?"

"Well, that's true," George said. "But I won't ask you for much. We're friends, so I'll lower the price."

"How much?" I asked him.

"Five thousand dollars," he said.

My heart sank. Here I was being offered a chance to have my own business, security for the children and myself. It would be more than just a job, it would be a future.

"I'm sorry," I told George. "I don't have that kind of money."

Five thousand might as well have been five million.

"Well," George continued and he was adamant. "I'm not going to give up on you. See if you can borrow the money somewhere. Maybe your mom could help out or something."

"I'll try," I said. "How long can you hold it for me? When do you have to know for sure?"

"Two weeks," he said. "I won't offer it to anyone else for two weeks."

Although I didn't hold out much hope for a miracle, my mind wouldn't let go of George's offer. To tell the truth, I was obsessed with it. I knew I could make a go of my own business if I just had the opportunity. Now here it was, a carrot being dangled under my nose, just beyond my reach, five thousand dollars away.

Forget it.

I told myself that maybe in a couple of years, when I was better off financially, something else might come along.

I put off calling George, though, as the two weeks were about gone. And then, one morning, mother called. I instantly knew it was bad news.

"Honey," she said, "your Uncle Larry has passed away."

Although he had been ill with cancer for some time, the news still hit me hard, as it did everyone in the family. Uncle Larry had been such a joy to all of us. But I could take solace that he was at peace now, his sickness had been a terrible thing.

Memories of Uncle Larry, my godfather, came flooding back to me. This dear old guy in his old-fashioned suits and shoes and hats—always so afraid to spend any money on himself, well, let's face it: spend any money, period. He was conservative through and through, Uncle Bing's dependable right arm for so many years.

He took me to Scandia back in the old days, bestowed all those "best joke" prizes on me at Uncle Bing's Pro-Am, and had, a scarce eight months before, hosted my children and me at his home in Los Angeles. We swam in his pool and he had presented us with tickets to Disneyland, an uncharacteristic extravagance that had been his way of saying goodbye.

Mother said she would get back to me regarding funeral arrangements, that things were being handled by his son and his attorney, who had phoned her with the news.

"I understand Larry remembered you in his will," mother said.

That came as a real surprise; he had already done so much for me during his life, he needn't have done anything else.

"What? He did?" I asked. "Oh my gosh, what a sweetheart!"

Mother said, "He left you five thousand dollars."

I almost fainted.

I would have a shop, after all, thanks to my godfather, who truly had looked after me, both in life and in death. He had left me just exactly enough.

I called George immediately and gave him the news, and then I set about making my plans, still marveling at Uncle Larry's generosity.

One day, I was musing about what to name my jewelry and curio shop. I wanted something with an Indian sound, certainly, but not something hokey.

It came to me in a flash, the nickname Uncle Larry had given his wife, Elaine was *White Feather,* and that's what I called it.

So I had the money for the shop, but nothing for display cases or merchandise. I decided to incorporate and offered some shares of the place to my mother. She loved the idea of being part-owner of a going concern, and gave me the funds I needed to get it going.

I opened for business on April Fools Day, 1977, hoping against hope that it wasn't an omen. As things turned out, it was not. White Feather did very well, I had the shop for twenty years and seldom did a day go by that I didn't whisper thanks to Uncle Larry for his final gift.

19. NOW IS THE HOUR

About six months after I had opened White Feather, mother called, sobbing this time. She asked if I had heard the news.

I said I hadn't.

She told me Uncle Bing had died.

I was stunned. I could barely speak, nor could she. We agreed to wait awhile, and talk again that evening when we had both calmed down enough to deal with the sudden heartbreak.

The reaction was worldwide, of course. Uncle Bing's demise led every newscast, punctuated every conversation. It was quite literally a sudden death. By most accounts, Bing had been doing well and had fully recovered from a fearful fall he had suffered from the stage of a Pasadena auditorium the preceding March. He had resumed performing concerts around the world, and recording with gusto.

Things were still going great guns when he suffered a massive heart attack after a round of golf in Spain, uttering his truly famous last words, "That was a great game, fellas."

When mother and I spoke again, I learned the funeral would be delayed for some time. Uncle Bing's body had to be returned to the United States, first of all, and because he had passed away overseas there were more than the usual number of forms and documents which had to be completed.

I asked mother to be sure to let me know when and where the services would be held, so that I could attend. The following week, we exchanged several phone calls to firm up my travel plans.

Then mother called with the news that the funeral would be private, very much so. The list of mourners was quite small, indeed, and I was not on it. In his will, Bing had limited the roster to immediate family only.

Mother and J.T. drove to Los Angeles and checked into a hotel. The very day they arrived, the *National Enquirer* was on the stands with a story about Bing's death, which carried a photo of him lying in his casket.

Our family was absolutely appalled. We all felt it was such a terrible thing to do, so crude and disrespectful. I couldn't help but flash back on the surreal obscenity that had been Aunt Dixie's graveside service in 1952, a media event without respect or consideration.

It, too, had capped one of the saddest episodes in our family's history.

Dixie's death wasn't a sudden shock, as Bing's was, but a slow wasting-away.

DIXIE LEE CROSBY
In a Coma for Five Days, Bing's Wife Passed Away Today;
He and Their Four Sons Were at Her Bedside

Dixie's death notice in the Las Angeles Harold Express

She was just 40 years old when she became gravely ill. Mother had received some phone calls from Uncle Bing, during which he told her Dixie was not well, and it was worrisome.

His darkest fears were confirmed in short order. Tests revealed Dixie was suffering from ovarian cancer, and it was advanced. She soon required hospitalization. Bing told mother it didn't look good, that he was afraid he was going to lose her.

In time, Aunt Dixie told her husband she wanted to be at home, and he wanted her to be there just as much.

Bing had committed to do a picture in Europe and he asked Paramount to let him out of the contract. But everyone, including Dixie's doctor, advised him to make the movie, *Little Boy Lost*, because if he cancelled the picture and stayed, it would frighten her. She would know she was near the end. Bing often has been criticized for deciding to go to Europe, but the truth of the matter is he was heeding the advice of people he trusted, even his son Gary agreed.

His time in Europe was short-lived, in any case. Ultimately, Dixie's condition worsened still, and she went into a coma. Bing returned, and called the boys home from school. They were all at the house during the last days of her life, with the doctor a constant visitor. Bing was supported by his brothers, and by two priests from his alma mater, Gonzaga University in Spokane, Washington.

Mother decided she wanted to be with Bing and the boys, too, and so she traveled to Los Angeles. She later told me that when the doctor at last advised Bing that Dixie was slipping away, he was devastated, absolutely wiped out.

LAST RITES FOR MRS. CROSBY—Bing Crosby, center background, and his twin sons, Dennis, foreground, and Phillip, left, follow casket of Dixie Lee Crosby into Church of Good Shepherd in Beverly Hills. Other two Crosby sons are out of picture to the left.

Dixie's funeral at Church of the Good Shepard, Los Angeles

The priests administered the last rites while Bing sat, inconsolable, at her bedside.

He regarded his wife's still form for a long time, and then went to a jewelry box on a nearby vanity table and took from it the simple gold band that he had married Dixie with more than two decades before, back when they were young and starting out.

He returned to her bedside and removed the glittering gold and diamond wedding ring that he had given her to replace that much simpler token, after he had established his successful career and could afford a more substantial representation of his love.

Uncle Bing knelt down and replaced that more lavish ring with the band he had originally slipped onto her finger, and said over and over, "Why didn't I understand? Why didn't I understand?"

And then Dixie was gone.

Mother sent for me to attend her funeral, which was in a very large church, filled to capacity and surrounded by fans, onlookers and the media. Mother and I sat with the rest of the family in the first few pews.

It was difficult even to glance at Uncle Bing. He looked terrible, his happy-go-lucky demeanor obliterated. He was pale and morose, a broken man who had literally lost the love of his life.

One of the most poignant moments in the service was when the priest ended his homily by turning to my uncle and saying, "Don't forget, Bing, that where the blue of the night meets the gold of the day, someone waits for you."

Bing's fans followed us in the procession to the cemetery, and I was surprised, dismayed, to be more accurate, at how some people behaved, like this was a show of some kind. There were women in hair curlers, pulling along children, people eating their lunches, or talking, some excitedly. It was surreal.

The press, no surprise, behaved little better.

My cousin Gary remembered the scene at the graveyard as a circus, not a service, with the entire Crosby clan jostled and shouted at. Cries of "How do you feel?" pierced the air.

At one point, the photographers pressed in close, and Uncle Bing was really shaken. I remember as he began to cry, one of the shutterbugs moved forward, getting down on one knee, carefully aiming his camera and trying to get a photograph of that tear falling down Bing's face. It was so heartbreaking, and so very, very rude.

A gravedigger had left a shovel laying nearby, and my Uncle Everett, surely on some mission from God, picked up the shovel and hit that photographer and cried, "For Godsake, leave the man alone!"

A quarter century later, as I looked with dismay and disbelief at the photograph of his body in the *Enquirer*, I realized that, even to the last, leaving Bing Crosby alone with his dignity was seldom a high priority for the Fourth Estate.

"Isn't there some place they draw the line?" I wondered aloud.

Apparently, there was not.

Uncle Bing's service took place in the wee hours of the morning, another gesture toward privacy, I suspect. The casket was placed in a very small room, more like a chapel, really, than a church. Although there was a row of chairs set up, most everyone in the sparse crowd chose to stand throughout the ceremony.

As I have said, attendance was strictly regulated. Mother was not allowed to be accompanied by her husband, J.T., nor was Uncle Bob allowed to bring his wife, June. Mourners also included Kathryn and her children, mother, Bing's loyal office staff, sans spouses, Bing and Dixie's four boys who were allowed to be accompanied by their wives, and a few others.

A very simple ceremony was what Uncle Bing had specified in his will. This time, his wishes were respected.

Although few were there to personally pay their respects, tributes were organized all over the world. Churches, clubs, groups of all faiths, fans young and old held their own memorials, in their own towns, and certainly in their own hearts. The outpouring of love and admiration for my uncle was felt from every country on the planet.

Uncle Bing was laid to rest at Holy Cross Cemetery in Los Angeles, beside Aunt Dixie. All four boys have joined them now, with Phil's passing in 2004.

Marion Massey tends Bing's gravesite

As was said of his seafaring ancestor Nathaniel, so let it be said of Harry Lillis "Bing" Crosby:
He died as he lived, and left us his good name.

AFTERWORD

Aren't You Glad You're You?

My Uncle Bob Crosby passed away in March of 1993, the last leaf on that branch of the family tree which included mother, Uncle Bing, Everett, Larry, Kay and Ted.

Their surviving children number about a dozen, so I have quite a roster of first cousins.

It occurred to me, as I sat in church while attending Uncle Bob's funeral in La Jolla, California, that my cousins and I rarely kept in contact with each other, and what a shame that was.

When I returned home, I sent letters to all of them, suggesting a long-overdue reunion.

Their response was very gratifying.

The cousins voted me chairperson of this little get-together, since I had been the one who opened my big mouth about it in the first place.

We gathered in October, 1994, at mother's home in Carmel. There were hugs all around and loads of very serious catching-up with some members of the clan whom we hadn't seen in years.

Aunt Kay's daughter, Marilyn, was there, as were Uncle Bob's children, Cathy and Kris; Ted's offspring, Katie, Sister Dolores, Howard and Edward, made the party. Everett's daughter Mary Sue was there, as was Larry's son, Jack. Gary told me he would be there, but his illness took him a couple of months before the event was held. We were disappointed that none of Bing's other children chose to attend, but perhaps next time, they will.

A few of us brought our own children, and it was good to see this new generation of Crosbys getting to know one another. I hope we will all continue to stay in touch, and that we will always feel grateful for the remarkable family that we are a part of.

In my zeal to keep Uncle Bing's memory alive and well, I'm always available and willing to share my thoughts with Crosby fans and the media. Therefore, when I received a call from BBC Radio in 1998, inquiring if I might discuss my uncle for a program they were planning, I was delighted to participate.

They produced a wonderful Christmas special featuring the life and music of my uncle, what a compliment it was to be asked to be a part of the effort.

And the band plays on. I find it amazing, Uncle Bing probably would, too, that, more than 25 years after his death, the tributes and memorials to him continue.

In May of 2003, Uncle Bing's alma mater, Gonzaga University, which boasts the largest collection of Bing Crosby memorabilia in existence, sponsored a symposium where I was invited to sit on a panel with Kathryn, Rich Little, and others, to offer remembrances and answer questions. Titled "A Celebration of His Life," it was a lovely event, and so well-attended by my uncle's admirers, young and old. The banquet on Saturday evening included an appearance by Frank Sinatra Jr. who recounted the friendship between his father and Uncle Bing. A highlight was a performance of Bing's hits from the 1930s and 40s by my cousin, Howard Crosby, and his band. Howard does a superb job keeping the music alive and swinging. While at Gonzaga that weekend, I had the unexpected pleasure of walking through the old Crosby home, on Sharp Avenue. It was haunting, in a way, to walk up the stairs where all seven Crosby kids had chased each other up and down. I roamed through the upstairs bedrooms trying to guess which one was my mother's. Back down on the first floor is the dinning room and entrance hall. I could just imagine Grandma calling out, "no roughhousing boys, go outside if you want to do that". And then there was the parlor, reserved for visitors like the priest and the banker, I suppose. In his boyhood school days, Uncle Bing walked to his classes at the university, just a couple of blocks away. Since that time however, the school has grown and expanded to the point that the campus now includes the Sharp Avenue property. The old Crosby house has been beautifully maintained and is home to the Gonzaga Alumni Association.

Uncle Bing did not finish college. He left after two years, I believe. But later on when he became a celebrity, quite a number of former students laid claim to being well acquainted with him. "My class at Gonzaga gets bigger every year," Bing jokingly told mother.

In the fall of 2003, my friend Linda sent me an article from *Nevada* magazine about Uncle Bing. Written by Lin Anderson, it recounted Bing's days at his ranch in Elko, with special emphasis on Christmas.

I learned that Elko's Northeastern Nevada Museum had an exhibit of Uncle Bing's memorabilia. I had never heard of the museum, but made a special trip to see it right after the holidays, and brought along a few things that both mother and I had stored away in cardboard boxes, odds and ends of memorabilia like sheet music, Christmas cards, photos, news clippings and the like.

Bing (with hand to mouth), Kathryn, Grandma Kate, Dennis, Phil, Uncle Ted and Aunt Margaret, Uncle Larry and Aunt Elaine at Gonzaga University attending the conferring of an Honorary Degree upon Bing

The museum staff went crazy. They loved everything I brought and vowed to put my things in their exhibit, which was rather sparse. I had no idea that this occasion would be a media event in Uncle Bing's old getaway, but I found myself being interviewed by KELK Radio and the *Elko Daily Free Press*, where I ended up being front page news the following day.

Uncle Bing once said that he didn't think he was the kind of star who would be remembered in years to come. "After all," he said, "I didn't create the excitement of an Elvis or a Sinatra."

Oh yeah? Some folks in Spokane and Elko would surely disagree.

The famous Levi tuxedos

The expanded exhibit at Northwestern Nevada Museum

I did not, on the other hand, attend a recent three-day symposium which was held at Hofstra University in New York, but I doubt I would have been of much assistance to them if I had. I understand this was a "scholarly study" devoted to the life and times of Bing Crosby. Since my scholarly days are behind me, I allowed my younger cousin Howard Crosby, Ted's son, to carry the banner for our generation at this academic function. Howard reported back to me that it was a great occasion and that I should have been there. Irving Berlin's daughter attended, as well as other luminaries, Bing fans and professor types.

From what I've read, these academic folks at Hofstra dissected, bisected and all but resurrected the dear man. I'm sort of brain-dead when it comes to this kind of skull session, where things are analyzed to death, but who am I to criticize these learned men and women who showed so much interest in Uncle Bing a quarter century after his death?

Bravo, gentlemen! My mortarboard is off to you!

EPILOGUE

Without a Song

Sometime during my young adult years, the name Russ Columbo came up in a conversation I had with my mother. She told me that Columbo was a singer and actor in Hollywood around the time uncle Bing was getting his music and film career going, the late 1920's and early 30's. As I recall, she said that Bing and Russ had a similar singing style. In fact, it was sort of a race or competition if you will, to see which one of them would stay the course and be the most popular with the people. Mother couldn't remember why Russ dropped out, but it was obvious by this time that Uncle Bing was the winner.

For several years I wondered what happened to Columbo and my curiosity was mounting. Ironically, one afternoon an oldies radio station announced that "today we're going to play a recording of Russ Columbo for you from our 1920's collection". The music started, the voice began singing and I stopped dead in my tracks. He sounded so much like Uncle Bing I almost couldn't tell the difference. How amazing I thought, that one man would out distance the other, or was it just the luck of the draw or the toss of a coin?

Now the time is present day and I'm preparing to write this book. I solicited the help of my cousin Jack, Larry's son, for some pictures he might loan me. He showed me a lovely photo of his mother that was taken by the well known Hollywood photographer Lansing Brown. Jack said that Brown had killed Russ Columbo, I was speechless. Upon recovery, I asked him what he knew about the incident. "According to my mom, Brown and Columbo were together having a chat and examining a hand gun. It accidentally fired while Brown was holding it and the bullet ricocheted off the edge of a table hitting Columbo, who died of the wound," Jack said.

Upon further research, I found a published news account which stated that Uncle Bing was actually a pallbearer at Columbo's funeral.

For a number of years afterward, some people in Hollywood would argue that Bing copied Columbo's singing style. However, in an interview with orchestra leader Gus Arnheim, he is quoted as saying that he settled the issue some thirty years ago. It was Arnheim, I believe, who gave Russ the early break he needed to gain popularity. Gus stated that he used to watch Russ watching Bing and that Columbo would then use some of Bing's delivery for himself. This story seems to make sense, as Bing was five years older than Russ, who died at the age of twenty six.

In any event, here we have a case of fate, or the gods, or whatever, touching the lives of two men on the road to fame . . . or Singapore . . . or Zanzibar . . . or Morocco . . . or . . . .

If you would like to purchase
a personally autographed copy of
"Me and Uncle Bing"
directly from the author, please contact::

Carolyn Schneider
%White Feather Publishing Company
9811 W. Charleston Blvd. # 2-185
Las Vegas, Nevada 89117, USA
Phone and Fax: (702) 240-2479
E-mail: artist71635@msn.com